# FOREIGN ASSISTANCE

## A View from the Private Sector

## Kenneth W. Thompson

UNIVERSITY
PRESS OF
AMERICA

Copyright © 1972 by
University of Notre Dame Press

Reprinted by arrangement with
University of Notre Dame Press

**University Press of America, Inc.**

P.O. Box 19101, Washington, D.C. 20036

Printed in the United States of America

Library of Congress Cataloging in Publication Data

Thompson, Kenneth W., 1921-
   Foreign assistance.

   Reprint. Originally published: Notre Dame :
University of Notre Dame Press, c1972.
   Includes bibliographical references and index.
   1. Economic assistance, American.   I. Title.
[HC60.T493  1983]        338.91'73       82-25091
ISBN 0-8191-2713-2 (pbk.)

*You work not for to-day, but for ever; not for this generation, but for every generation of humanity that shall come after you.*

Frederick T. Gates

# CONTENTS

# ABBREVIATIONS

AID —Agency for International Development

BAPPENAS —National Planning Agency of Indonesia

CIMMYT —International Maize and Wheat Improvement Center (Centro Internacional de Mejoramiento de Maiz y Trigo)

CIAT —International Center of Tropical Agriculture (Centro Internacional de Agricultura Tropical)

FAO —Food and Agricultural Organization of the United Nations

ICA —International Cooperation Agency

IDS —Institute of Development Studies (Kenya)

IHD —International Health Division

IRRI —International Rice Research Institute

OECD —Organization for Economic Cooperation and Development

UNICEF —United Nations Children's Fund

UNO —United Nations Organization

WHO —World Health Organization

# PREFACE

This little book is intended to fill a vacuum in the literature on foreign assistance. Much has been written about national and international programs in foreign aid. Far less has been said about activities in the private sector, yet they have a long and worthy history. More importantly, they provide chapters in foreign aid in which we can trace how the story came out. They also permit generalization and statements about the underlying principles on which they were based.

Too little has been said in any context about the theory of foreign aid. In every annual debate accompanying the work of congressional committees, the tacit assumption of spokesmen is that foreign aid is good, while the opponents of aid take the line that it is harmful to our interests, wins no friends, and leads to involvement and war.

In thinking about foreign aid Americans should be able to examine the soundness of our objectives and measure our achievements against them. We should test the validity of certain concepts and precepts that provide working guides to policy. We ought to be able to analyze successes and failures in aid and trace some of the reasons why. It ought not to be impossible to relate institution-building to lessons from the past where single individuals or disciplines were the focus for our efforts and projects.

An old-fashioned idea underlies this book and the

themes that flow in and through it. Phrased in ancient and respected terms, it is that for powerful men and nations "from him to whom much is given, from him shall much be expected." When all is said and done, and every rational argument adduced, the core justification for foreign aid is the moral imperative that the rich ought to help the poor.

Modern civilization, embarrassed by the pretentiousness of most moralistic rhetoric, has thrown off not only the excesses of moralism but the abiding truths of morality, and this may be the cause for the decline of support for foreign aid. The inescapable fact of life in every community, whether the family or the world, is that we need one another. Yet we don't understand one another; we hurt one another. Interdependency and dependency, which are both essential, are equally fraught with psychological perils. In the face of these perils, if there is any cure for our tendency to draw apart, it is through actually working together. There is a profound moral center to every serious effort at international cooperation whereby men seek to become what by their nature they are capable of being but are denied by all the forces that pull us apart.

I have drawn more heavily on the experience of one institution in the private sector than some may feel warranted. I have done so deliberately, however, because its living history is known to me intellectually and in my bones as no other experience in foreign assistance. For almost two decades I have immersed myself in its purposes, programs, and problems. I have been soaked in its history through the words and reflections of men who struggled to bring change into being. Through concentrating on what is known, I have tried to move out to what were for me less well known but no less significant efforts of other institutions.

I hope this study will stimulate others to extend their work in this vital and significant field and to explore dimensions that have fallen beyond my competence and authority. Since this is a book intended to provoke thought and discussion, not necessarily to offer solutions, the focus I have taken is that of a personal statement. My views do not reflect those of any institution, and I take full responsibility for the conclusions.

I am especially indebted to Helen Danner, who assisted throughout in the editing, revising, and typing of the manuscript, and to Catherine Kapoor, who in the earlier stages was equally helpful. Each is an extraordinarily able and cultured person who combines intellectual with technical skills. I am also grateful to my colleague Dr. Michael P. Todaro, who reviewed the entire manuscript and provided major assistance on the Economics chapter. Dr. Clarence C. Gray III and Dr. Virgil C. Scott were also most helpful. I owe an immense debt to the Hazen Foundation, which organized discussions at which some of the major themes were aired. Dr. Paul Braisted in particular has been supportive and understanding. But none of these trusted friends bears any responsibility for the shortcomings of the volume, for which I alone am accountable.

K.W.T.

New York, New York
January 1972

# 1: PRIVATE ASSETS IN INTERNATIONAL COOPERATION

Foreign assistance in America has fallen on evil days. The signs of the times for those who believe in aid are sobering. According to a recent poll, an increasingly smaller percentage of the population favors giving foreign assistance to other nations. An increasingly larger group doubts the efficacy of our assistance to other nations. The point is increasingly made that after billions of dollars expended around the world we have fewer friends, indeed that our aid has gained us more adversaries than allies. A liberal senator whose name for more than two decades had been synonymous with international cooperation turns critic and warns that foreign assistance leads to military commitments and war. In the 1960's the curve of annual appropriations for foreign assistance moved steadily downward and the bright glow of moral fervor that surrounded international cooperation faded into the dull gray of skepticism, opposition, and doubt. Even a series of distinguished committees that have evaluated and reformulated approaches and machinery for the management of foreign aid have thus far not succeeded in turning the tide. As if to cap this trend, the Senate in

November 1971, for the first time in its history, rejected legislation put forward by the Nixon administration and foreign aid funding at that point was placed on a week to week basis.

What are the reasons for this decline and for the loss of popular enthusiasm and support? Surely one all pervasive element is the national mood and psychology, intensified and brought into focus by Vietnam, but having a long and melancholy history of its own. An atmosphere of weariness, disappointment, and *malaise* has fallen over the nation—understandable perhaps following a quarter century of struggle and sacrifice to build a better world. We are living in "the winter of our discontent." The seeds of disillusionment were planted by those who oversold international cooperation, only to have the mortgage come due in a world that remained troubled and essentially unchanged. The claims and justification for aid had varied from assertions that foreign aid would put an end to selfish nationalism, to promises that it would turn back world communism, to prophecies that it would usher in a new and better world. In justifying foreign aid its champions, in short, claimed more than was realistic. However, utopianism has been only one of the dominant philosophies of foreign aid. It has also been linked by many supporters, too narrowly it seems, with national security and military defense. For a time military assistance carried economic assistance in a militantly anticommunist Congress. Through assistance to those on the front line of freedom we were to escape the necessity of fighting ourselves. According to critics in the Senate Foreign

2

Relations Committee, this assumption has been tried and found wanting on the battlefields of Vietnam.

Disenchantment with foreign assistance also stems from the widespread and unrelenting publicity given to our failures. The mass media and certain journalists have subjected to pitiless publicity foreign assistance projects that miscarried, and have been joined by congressional committees that, as watchdogs of public finance, have singled out egregious cases of misuse of taxpayers' resources. Far less has been written about the quiet successes that are equally part of the story. It is frequently asserted by Washington observers that foreign aid has no political constituency and that foreigners don't vote. In any event, support for international cooperation today lacks political sex appeal, and fewer and fewer politicians have been prepared to stake their careers on its sponsorship.

It is the first thesis of this book that at least part of the problem is ignorance about what is being done. One important form of assistance that seldom makes headlines in international cooperation is that emanating from the private sector. To single out private assistance is in no sense to propose it as an alternative. Its interrelationship with efforts in the public sector would carry us beyond the present study. Suffice it to say privately funded experiments are often designed from the start to allow public takeover if they succeed. Without disparaging the merits of public programs, long-term endeavors in private foreign aid require study that is long overdue.

In the crisis over foreign assistance, the light which

private programs throw on recurrent problems could be helpful. They have had a long history, going back to the turn of the century and beyond. In their formulation and administration, they reflect a rich and ample body of experience. It would not be claiming too much to assert that they have had some not inconsiderable successes. Many leaders are still in the field and have lived and worked for long periods with nationals of other countries. Their programs have evolved and, more than newer public programs, illustrate an evolving pattern of response to urgent human needs. A literature has grown up around them, and their records are open and awaiting study and review. Some chapters in the story are now closed and it is possible to trace them with all their advances, false starts, and setbacks through a beginning, middle and end. They have alumni, past and present leaders, and theories about the recruitment, assignment, and use of leadership. There is foundation lore and, unhappily, foundation jargon. Concepts and precepts abound and the present study recites those which the author knows best and whose application has been a part of his life and work. Some years ago, Dr. Henry Kissinger wrote of the need for a doctrine of national security, and it may be legitimate to ask whether we have operated from anything approaching a doctrine or set of doctrines about foreign assistance.

It would be pretentious for anyone to speak for the broad and varied realm of foreign assistance. The imperatives and objectives vary across a wide spectrum of international, bilateral and myriad voluntary undertak-

4

ings. The context within which a United Nations agency, the State Department or the Agency for International Development, or Church World Service operate differs to the point of being different in kind. German, British, Israeli, or Japanese foreign assistance programs, and France with its "mission civilisatrice" are impelled by goals and administered through organizations and by techniques that diverge more radically still from agencies in the American context.

Moreover, pride in the ventures with which one is familiar may tempt to chauvinism and self-righteousness —traits from which executors of foreign assistance are plainly not immune. An incredible amount of human energy can be devoted by "operators" in the name of international cooperation to differentiating between "we" and "they." Behind every successful experiment there is a necessary amount of institutional pride. Identity is as vital to cooperative activities in foreign aid as to any other form of group activity. The hazard of group pride, however, is that it is but one step removed from parochialism and narrow-mindedness. It can divide when the needs to be served call for unity and collaboration. Warring tribes of foreign assistance agencies provide the surest guarantee of failure, and while for recipients there may be passing attraction in such divisions and a temptation to play donors off against one another, the long-term effects, given urgent needs, will be little short of disastrous.

Therefore, my intention in discussing the private sector is not to set it apart as morally superior to all other types of foreign assistance. International cooperation to assist in the solution of urgent and pressing problems ought to be a seamless web. The part of the total which private agencies contribute inevitably will be a fraction of the whole. This has not always been the case, anymore than on the domestic scene. The Rockefeller Foundation was unique in its early assistance to medical education, medical research, and schools of public health, but today it has been supplanted by large-scale assistance from the National Science Foundation and the National Institutes of Health. When the International Health Division launched its war against disease it had few partners, but today national and international organizations have taken over the task. Parochialism for private institutions is a contradiction in terms given the need for ever-expanding resources and the mission of helping and working together with all mankind.

The sense of urgency required further precludes this attitude. Famine and overpopulation cannot wait for the resolution of jurisdictional disputes or the arbitration of petty and selfish squabbles. History and the demands for problem-solving have been telescoped into an ever-shorter time span; business as usual is an anachronism in the 1970's. England could afford slow-paced progress and Japan a long period of isolation in their development. India or Indonesia are denied this and so are those who would provide help. It will not do to study a problem to death or to proceed along divergent lines in the hope that they will ultimately converge.

Therefore, those who labor in the private sector have learned by trial and error the necessity of working

6

together. Today there are rays of hope in the skies over Indian agricultural development because AID, the Ford and the Rockefeller Foundations have dovetailed their separate efforts to bring about a common goal: Rockefeller with its new wheat and rice varieties and packages of practices, Ford with community projects that have brought scientific agriculture to the people, and AID with seed factories and fertilizer plants essential to exploiting the new technology. One without the other would have delayed or prevented the birth of "the green revolution." Taken together they have assured that through its initiative India has been given the chance to march forward toward agricultural self-sufficiency. Equally, the successes of the International Rice Research Institute would be inconceivable without the cooperation of these same bodies, plus the United Nations, the World Bank, and national programs, such as Canadian technical assistance.

Need and urgency, therefore, have become correctives to overweening self-righteousness and particularism. There is no substitute for agencies working together on a common problem nor for a recognition that others have something unique to offer. Yet differences in modes of operation, size and scale of resources, style and tenure of the "operators," and the accidents of circumstances and relationships in the country men seek to help can all stand in the way of genuine and wholehearted cooperation. "Pride and ambition," Winston Churchill declared, "are the prod and goal of every worthwhile accomplishment." We cannot do without them. Yet pride can be the

7

route either to a sense of overweaning superiority that breeds hostility and suspicion or to strengthening institutional self-confidence, which can open up broad avenues of trust and collaboration. Thucydides, writing of the relationship between the ancient Greek city-states, observed "there can be no justice among unequals" and the paraphrase follows logically: "nor cooperation."

This is the rationale for a clear-cut and forceful statement of what can be expected from private initiative in foreign assistance. There would be little point in discussing the private area in foreign assistance unless we were convinced it had lessons for foreign aid in general. Those who are closest to its history and record have pride in its accomplishment and ambition to see it improved. Yet no one can be oblivious to its limitations and those substantial differences in opportunities and procedures that set it apart. Knowing this may help the reader to place what follows in perspective and balance.

The enumeration of private assets in foreign assistance must begin with the peculiar and unique character of the private foundation. In a word, it is a national institution with international purposes. Its concern is with humanity as a whole. Frederick T. Gates, the Baptist minister who became John D. Rockefeller's principal advisor, asked in 1911: "Is there not something within us, an instinct, which is the harbinger perhaps of better things, an instinct of humanity, which cannot be fenced in by the boundaries of a merely national patriotism, a sympathy which transcends national boundaries and which finds complete expression only when it identifies us with all humanity?"[1] This vision of the future was written into the charter of the Rockefeller Foundation, which spoke of serving "the well-being," not of Americans or southerners or minorities alone, but of "mankind throughout the world." This has never meant freedom from public accountability to the nation nor the absence of a public trust. As early as 1913, Jerome D. Greene, its first executive secretary, spoke of "the accountability of The Rockefeller Foundation to the people of the United States" and sought ways it could benefit from "public scrutiny, criticism and publicity."[2] In relation to great national purposes it was "an extra engine put on to help the nation over a stiff grade."[3] As one step in meeting its accountability to the nation, the Foundation initiated a system of annual reports that would lay bare to the public its purposes, assets, appropriations, and payments. The provision of public reporting which nearly six decades later was written into the law of the land was instituted from birth by the Foundation.

What are the roots of this worldwide mission? Unquestionably, for some the universality of the Foundation's mandate was inseparably linked with a religious heritage. The resolution by which the trustees moved to project around the globe the hookworm work of the old Rocke-

[1] The Frederick T. Gates Collection, Rockefeller Foundation Archives, An Address on the 10th Anniversary of the [Rockefeller] Institute [for Medical Research], 1911.

[2] Raymond B. Fosdick, *The Story of The Rockefeller Foundation* (New York: Harper & Brothers, 1952), p. 290.

[3] *Ibid.*

feller Sanitary Commission—work which at its inception had been limited to the South—called to mind for at least one trustee "a response to the same entreaty which had greeted St. Paul: 'Come over into Macedonia and help us.' "[4] For others more rationalist than religious in their thinking and believing that knowledge was the patrimony not of nations but of humanity, the war against disease and suffering required a common front drawing on the resources of all countries. The peoples of the world had to face the enemies of mankind, not as isolated groups behind national boundaries, but as members of the human race in frightening propinquity to disaster.

In his president's review of 1941, Raymond Fosdick described the common fund of knowledge and that invisible host of scientists who never thought of flags or boundaries nor served a lesser loyalty than the welfare of mankind. He saw men everywhere, from birth to death and in war or peace alike, as beneficiaries of knowledge, for no nation has a monopoly on discovery or excellence. Internationalism for Fosdick had a wholly practical basis, for in war:

> An American soldier wounded on a battlefield in the Far East owes his life to the Japanese scientist, Kitasato, who isolated the bacillus of tetanus. A Russian soldier saved by a blood transfusion is indebted to Landsteiner, an Austrian. A German soldier is shielded from typhoid fever with the help of a Russian, Metchnikoff. A Dutch marine in the East Indies is protected from malaria because of the experiments of an Italian, Grassi; while a

[4] *Ibid.*, p. 279.

> British aviator in North Africa escapes death from surgical infection because a Frenchman, Pasteur, and a German, Koch, elaborated a new technique.

And in peace:

> Our children are guarded from diphtheria by what a Japanese and a German did; they are protected from smallpox by an Englishman's work; they are saved from rabies because of a Frenchman; they are cured of pellagra through the researches of an Austrian.[5]

Through its history, the Foundation has established contacts with more than a hundred countries, territories, or political units in the world, sometimes directly but often through the agencies it has supported. Led by its medical scientists, for whom there were few political constraints, the Foundation pursued its doctrine of universality deriving from the twin sources of theology and reason, or from the New Testament and the Graeco-Roman traditions.

Yet this high faith in a common destiny, which undergirds cooperation with others and which may be the most powerful and inspiring doctrine in the history of foreign assistance, has met two serious limitations. The one has its locus outside the foundation—in the conditions of international society. During and following World War II, the dark clouds of conflict hung over international cooperation and overtures to many nations fell on deaf ears. Surveying the postwar era, Fosdick wrote more

[5] *The Rockefeller Foundation Annual Report*—1941, President's Review, p. 10.

in hope than assurance: "perhaps it is not too much to hope that some new pattern will evolve, some internal regeneration among the people of the Soviet Union, which will open their doors and windows to the stimulus of ideas from without, and . . . come like a clear breeze to refresh the spirits and minds of men."[6] In recent months, a similar hope for change within Communist China has been born and with it renewed faith in universality, embodied of course in the seating of their delegates at the UN. Yet while men live in one world, that world is still comprised of struggling and contending sovereign states pitted against one another by profound ideological and political differences.

The other constraint comes from the need to concentrate scarce resources in precisely defined areas of need. The late President Francis Keppel of the Carnegie Corporation observed: "In philanthropy as in baseball, you score runs by bunching hits." Much of established doctrine in private foreign assistance revolves around the principle of concentrating efforts. Ways have to be found to capitalize on scarce resources. Most basic is the principle that the goal should be to give assistance to projects that deal with root causes, not symptoms. The focus is on problems that lie at the root of human difficulties and require patience, tenacity, research, careful planning, and adequate and continuing funds. The temptation is always scatteration or the frittering away of monies in an endless series of small grants. The balancing truth is that

[6] Fosdick, p. 288.

12

it is better to begin in a small way and progress by trial and error toward larger ends. There is heartache bound up with concentrating on root causes, for in the words of an early philanthropist: "To help the sick and distressed appeals to the kind-hearted always. But to help the investigator who is striving successfully to attack the causes that bring about sickness and distress does not so strongly attract the giver of money."[7]

A final expression of the idea of making limited resources pay off is the need to be ever vigilant to new opportunities and responsive to changing human need. Flexibility in initiating must be matched by flexibility in terminating. The primary objective of a general purpose foundation is to prime the pump, never to act as a permanent reservoir for a single enterprise. Grants and policies should not be tied to rigid and unchangeable purposes or ruled by "the dead hand of the past." Foundations with a broad mandate must be free to pursue each vital program activity to a logical conclusion and to turn their attention to the next urgent and emerging challenge to which they feel able to contribute and respond. In this regard, great advantages accrue from an elastic charter and the assignment of responsibility to present trustees to identify and encourage new approaches to new and urgent human needs. It is important to retain a healthy skepticism about the ability of one generation to foresee the needs and requirements of the next.

To those who live and labor in the private sector,

---

[7] *Ibid.*, p. 296.

working principles such as those enumerated above carry weight and meaning, and provide the basic elements of a living creed. For outsiders, they may appear no more than truisms or self-evident statements, without the force of first principles or informing concepts. It is instructive therefore to invite the skeptic to examine both the principles and their possible application in the context of international political life. Foreign assistance in the public sphere is subject to myriad pressures and constraints, often written into legislation, that are generally unknown to the private sector. It is noble to talk about projects that focus on root causes but who if not mutual assistance agencies will resist hostile guerilla forces sweeping across national frontiers and threatening a friendly government? It is one thing for a private body to speak of concentrating resources but the government of the United States has diplomatic relations with 123 proud and sensitive nation-states. And what does the principle of freedom and unchangeable purposes mean to responsible public leaders who year after year face the prospect that a strategically important government will fall unless we balance our own assistance against the aid pouring in to its enemies from unfriendly powers? If these examples are instances in the extreme, they are notwithstanding part of the realities of foreign assistance governed by short-run political and foreign-policy imperatives.

It could be that the greatest asset of the private sector is its relative freedom from these all controlling strategic and geo-political constraints. Dean Rusk in his days as a foundation executive reminded his colleagues that they operated from "a packed suitcase." If they had fulfilled their mission, were unable to function and contribute effectively, or found themselves hampered by a breach of the working agreement, they could pack up and leave without risking a diplomatic incident. It would be stretching a point to claim they are never judged as Americans, but that judgment is tempered because they also represent an international foundation.

The position of the international foundation with a long-standing world mission is therefore a priceless legacy in countries around the world, and particularly in those most sensitive to intrusion of American power. But there is another asset less widely known but equally valuable. A corollary of the opportunity to change and of flexibility in shifting programs to meet urgent emerging needs is the continuity of experience and the unfolding of personal and professional relations of foundation leaders abroad. For the Rockefeller Foundation, medical and public health men paved the way for agriculturalists in South America and Asia. The work of agriculturalists in turn gives credibility to populationists, social scientists, and others who follow them. Wherever a Foundation officer goes today, the odds are good that a predecessor has cleared a path through the thickets of ignorance and mistrust that so often impede international cooperation.

Private assets in foreign assistance are resources for international cooperation more highly prized than large-scale investments in human and material capital. Inevitably comparisons come to mind, such as the question: How can it be that a mere handful of men were able to accomplish what hundreds later on failed to do? Part of the answer has to be time and circumstances. "For everything there is a season." The time was ripe for the little band of medical scientists who made up the contingents in Asia and South America and carried forward the mission of the International Health Division. "A time to plant and a time to pluck up." The 1940's and 1950's were a time for the Rockefeller Foundation agricultural staff to join with fledgling scientists in Mexico to turn corn and wheat production around in Mexico. "A time to learn and a time to give back." Mexico in the 1960's became the home of an international center that reaches out to help others. And in the 1960's, it was a time for institution building and for visiting Rockefeller Foundation staff to serve as deans and department heads in university development centers in Africa, Latin America, and Asia. Now, with nationalism intensifying in many developing countries, the time may have passed when direct and visible leadership is possible—but once again a flexible response is both possible and necessary.

It is also true that foreign assistance needs can eclipse the potential of private resources. The private institution, however noble its purpose and well-qualified its professional staff, may be obliged to hand over the task to larger national and international institutions. At certain stages in development, pump priming is not enough. At this moment, the private body can hope that its experience may be of some value to others, but the context of public assistance may set limits to any such transfer of knowledge. The processes of establishing priorities, justi-

16

fying expenditures, and sustaining efforts can be quite different in the public sector.

Nevertheless, there are lessons that need not be confined to particular private organizations. If communications between the private and public sectors leave something to be desired, it is tragically apparent that intercommunication within the private sector, given its diversity and differences, has often been woefully inadequate. "Physician, heal thyself" is a motto that those engaged in private initiatives might appropriate themselves.

The test of the value of private assets must be made at the level of application and practice; it will never be resolved theoretically. For those who have applied them within the context of concrete programs and objectives, there is little debate over their relevance and validity. The most useful contribution we can make is to lay before the reader what has happened in health, agriculture, economics, and university development and leave to others inquiries in different spheres. And it may be that a fuller elaboration of concepts and precepts of private foreign assistance will make more specific the ways in which cooperation can unfold. I propose to examine these dimensions of private foreign assistance in the chapters that follow.

# 2: HEALTH AS THE EARLIEST CHAPTER

Looking back on the early history of foreign assistance in the private sector, an air of predetermination hung over the focus and thrust it was to take. In vast areas of the United States and across the world, the problem of disease stood out in stark relief as "the supreme ill of human life" and as "the main source of almost all other ills—poverty, crime, ignorance, vice, inefficiency, hereditary taint, and many other evils."[1] It was an area in which it was possible, as was less true in social relations, to search out the root cause, to cure evils at their source. There was a body of knowledge on which to build and some experience in applying it in regions of greatest need. The Rockefeller Sanitary Commission had achieved dramatic success in greatly reducing hookworm in the southern United States, and the stated objective of the International Health Board, created by the Rockefeller Foundation in 1913, was "to extend to other countries and peoples the work of eradicating Hookworm Disease

[1] Frederick T. Gates, "Philosophy & Civilization," 1923. The Frederick T. Gates Collection, Rockefeller Foundation Archives (Gates on Policy 1905–26, pp. 16–17).

as opportunity offers. . . ."[2] This board and its successor organizations, culminating in the International Health Division (established in 1927), sought to promote the spread of scientific medicine and to support or establish agencies for the promotion of public sanitation. The scope of the effort coincided with the international mandate of the Rockefeller Foundation. It was also to exemplify the dividends of concentration and of pursuing a clear-cut goal with singularity of purpose. There was a recognized need and the prospect of solutions in the field could be envisaged from work already in progress at the more advanced centers.

Hookworm is an anemia-producing disease contracted by contact with infected soil (especially through bare feet), which in that era handicapped, debilitated and killed millions of people in the hot, humid regions of the world. In rural areas of the South, the percentage of infected children ran as high as 90 percent, with the incidence among adults also high. The objective of the first phase of the campaign was to demonstrate that hookworm was a reality, a source of debilitation and weakness, but at the same time curable and preventable. The task of the Rockefeller Sanitary Commission was to educate and to curb lethargy and indifference, including that of the medical profession. If illness is the supreme ill, bad health, like the weather, is many times accepted as inevitable.

[2] Minutes of The Rockefeller Foundation, June 27, 1913, p. 1027.

Here was the classic instance of a private agency playing a catalytic and educational role. The Sanitary Commission appointed directors of sanitation in each of the eleven states in which work was undertaken. Traveling dispensaries brought knowledge to the people. The schools were enlisted, as were state departments of education. Capsules of thymol and salts, a form of medication since outdated, were distributed after medical examinations, lectures, and demonstrations. More than 250,000 rural homes were inspected by sanitary personnel, and measures, in particular the construction of sanitary privies, were instituted to prevent recurrence of the disease. Over 25,000 public meetings were held with attendance exceeding two million people in 653 of the 1,142 counties in eleven southern states. Voluntary groups in the state such as women's clubs and school improvement leagues were formed and an immense cooperative effort conducted between state and county governments and the Sanitary Commission. As a harbinger of future patterns of international cooperation, the professional staff everywhere functioned under state control. The commission leader, Dr. Wickliffe Rose, wrote: "The eradication of this disease . . . is a work which no outside agency working independently could do for a people if it would, and . . . no outside agency should do if it could."[3]

The leadership of the Sanitary Commission was imbued with an international outlook even before it merged

[3] The Rockefeller Sanitary Commission for the Eradication of Hookwork Disease: Organization, Activities and Results up to December 31, 1910, p. 4.

in 1913 with the Rockefeller Foundation as the International Health Board. One reason was that medical science was universal and knew no boundaries. Inquiries through government agencies in Washington and abroad established the fact that hookworm extended around the world from approximately the thirty-sixth parallel north to the thirtieth parallel south, involving a population of a billion people. The work of the International Health Board in its war against hookworm reached out to fifty-two countries on six continents and to twenty-nine islands, extending from Fiji and Samoa westward through the Antipodes and the Far East to Africa and the Mediterranean and on to the West Indies and the Americas. The board had an operating model. Wherever it went it sought to apply the lessons of the Sanitary Commission: to work through established and responsible indigenous institutions, to ask that governments contribute, and to be "a partner, but not a patron." In Dr. Rose's enduring phrase:

> Demonstrations in which the . . . authorities do not participate . . . from the inception . . . are not likely to be successful; . . . the state must be sufficiently interested to risk something, to follow the plan critically, to take over the cost of the work gradually but steadily, and within a reasonable period to assume the entire burden of direction and expense.[4]

For today's practitioners of foreign assistance, the early

---

[4] *The Rockefeller Foundation Annual Report—1923*, p. 88.

22

formulation of this principle suggests there is nothing new under the sun.

From the start, the International Health Board followed another course that was to become the hallmark of private initiative. It sought to attract and hold the ablest young professionals as part of a cadre of career servants. These men were to write history in the public health area and to live out their lives or substantial parts thereof in far-flung corners of the world: Dr. Victor G. Heiser in the Far East; Dr. S. M. Lambert in Fiji, Samoa, and Polynesia; Dr. Wilbur A. Sawyer in Australia; Dr. George K. Strode in Brazil; and others, like Dr. Lewis W. Hackett and Dr. Charles N. Leach. The success of the board and of its successor, the International Health Division, would have been impossible without these legendary figures and the young scientists who developed under their tutelage.

The International Health Division ranged over the world for thirty-eight years. Its staff, which numbered annually seventy to eighty professionals—just about the size of the Foundation's agricultural staff three decades later—worked with seventy-five cooperating governments. It broadened its approach to include twenty-one specific diseases or health problems, including tuberculosis, yaws, rabies, influenza, typhus, amebiasis, schistosomiasis, dysentery, typhoid fever, hepatitis, undulant fever, and nutritional deficiencies. But in keeping with the concept of focus, the three major prongs of its efforts were hookworm, malaria, and yellow fever.

The IHD learned from doing and through trial and

error. For example, in hookworm, the staff early in its Asian efforts treated people en masse on the theory that in hookworm control the essential objective was less to cure each infected person than to remove the largest number of worms from the largest possible number of people, thus lowering the severity of infection. In the Dutch East Indies, India, Thailand, and other heavily infected tropical countries this mass approach supplanted the procedure of individual examinations which had been taken over from the Sanitary Commission. Later, mass treatments in turn were abandoned and emphasis was placed on improved sanitary arrangements and treatment only of those persons who were seriously infected. Laboratory tests had shown that some individuals carrying a small number of hookworms were not necessarily ill, that through the workings of antibodies many had relatively harmless infections and had acquired immunity to future infection even though constantly exposed to infecting larvae. A distinction came to be made between hookworm disease and harmless infection.

A final shift of emphasis in the hookworm campaign was to drop the term "eradication." It remains, as with "total solutions" to most human needs, a goal that has never been reached. Advocacy in foreign assistance, as in politics, leads to overstatement, and private enterprises are not immune. The battle cries are unequivocal: the conquest of hunger, eradication of disease, etc. Results inescapably fall short of the goal, but there is probably virtue in formulating human goals that exceed man's grasp. The prevalence of hookworm, in the end, was drastically limited so that today, like smallpox and typhoid, it is subject to control by modern public health methods.

The lore and legend, myths and miracles, triumphs and tragedies encountered in moving ahead with world health could fill volumes. Some stories are particularly well known and often told. Dr. Wilfred E. Barnes in Siam encountered a Buddhist priest forbidden by his religion to take life and therefore resistant to anything that would "kill the germs." Finally Barnes, having been rebuffed on every other ground, persuaded the priest to take hookworm medicine by displaying the washings from the stool that showed the worms were still alive when expelled. Dr. Lambert, in his work in Polynesia and Micronesia, found the Papuans reticent to give their names for labels on specimens, lest in speaking their names aloud the spirit of a dead relative would hear and come back to haunt them. The problem was solved by having the individual whisper his name to a bystander, who passed it on—also in a whisper. And there were a thousand more encounters with the folklore and the faith of other peoples.

There was also the eternal debate over research. At first, Rose and his associates assumed that eradication would take place through the application of known scientific methods. Experience put question marks after this assumption. A debate broke out within the IHD, with men like Dr. Simon Flexner, director of the Rockefeller Institute for Medical Research, asserting that the IHD was not a research organization and others, like Dr.

William H. Welch, the first dean of the Johns Hopkins Medical School, calling for a joint Johns Hopkins–Rockefeller Foundation twenty-year program of "wormology." In this debate, the researchers won out and studies at Johns Hopkins and in field and laboratory stations continued well into the 1940's. They included investigations of the interplay between man's relative immunity and his nutritional balance and the discovery of a hookworm egg-counting technique that enabled doctors to estimate the number of worms in a patient from the number of eggs in one gram of his feces. Men like Frederick F. Russell, a giant in the medical sciences, were impressed with the gap, not between scientific knowledge and its application, but between what science knew and what it needed to know.

The IHD remained essentially a field program and operating agency but was flexible enough to support and draw upon other scientific institutions in doing needed research. Again and again this has been the case with operating programs abroad, and those who disparage research in the name of action have been as wrong as those who call only for research. In all realism we must hasten to add that for the most part the research left the plight of barefoot, hookworm-infected humanity where it found it. No one discovered a simple vaccine or a soil disinfectant, and the gains in hookworm control went on within defined and narrow limits.

It must have been tempting along the way for the doctors, as with population specialists today, to feel discouraged, defeated, and depressed. Yet in the end, the results were impressive. A study of fifty-two counties in Mississippi showed that hookworm had been reduced by two-thirds between 1910 and 1933. A companion study in eight southern states disclosed a similar overall trend but with substantial residual pockets of resistance persisting along the sandy coastal plains from North Carolina to Mississippi. Outside these areas, if hookworm has not been eradicated, the disease is rarely seen. Although it still has not died out, no one today considers it more than a minor problem. But what was the cause of this change, or the causes? Was it the education of local doctors, increased incomes for the purchase of shoes, the drift to the cities, improved diets, or the catalytic effect of the IHD? Undoubtedly the answer is that it was a combination of medical, economic, and social factors, but a further question worth asking is whether these energies would have been unleashed in the absence of an organizing driving force such as the IHD.

Worldwide, the picture is less clear in the absence of convincing statistics and the geographical sprawl across six continents. One estimate indicated that more than six hundred million people are still infected, but this must be balanced against the fact that a study of tropical health published in the 1960's ranks hookworm ninth in cases reported (in a survey population of 1.2 million) and twenty-third as a cause of death. Further progress depends as much on breakthroughs in nutrition as on advances in the always difficult sanitation field because it appears self-evident today that the quality of food consumption is related to susceptibility to disease. To have discovered

27

this, an organization had to be active and alert on a broad social and scientific front, not narrowly concentrated on the cause and prevention of disease.

Once again, we can ask what might have been the out-lines of the problem if a private agency with a modicum of national success had not extended its efforts to the world at large. The strength of the Rockefeller Founda-tion, as of its International Health Division, is the ability of its staff to move back and forth, now within the terri-torial limits of a scientifically advanced country, now in some of the least developed countries of the world. It is stronger because it is a national institution with an inter-national outreach than if either of these elements were lacking. Understanding the cultural context in which health problems exist can be as vital as understanding their epidemiology. It is difficult enough to understand one's own culture and the interplay of social, economic, and health factors within it. How much more difficult to penetrate the enormously complicated layers of culture in other lands. In the words of Dr. John B. Grant, who served in China, India, and Puerto Rico: "Technical solu-tions to health problems should be humanized by an understanding of the existing cultures and subcultures and the ways these are changing."[5] Only a body of men who combine love for medicine with love for foreign cul-tures would be capable of penetrating these subtle realms.

[5] Conrad Seip, ed., *Health Care for the Community: Selected Papers of Dr. John B. Grant* (Baltimore: Johns Hopkins Press, 1963), p. 178.

Yet something more was involved than the knowledge of a foreign culture or a single disease. From the outset, the war against hookworm was seen as important in itself but even more as "an advance agent of preventive medicine." It was both an end in itself and a means to a larger end. It was a demonstration project in disease control; and if it could succeed, the doctors in the IHD had faith that the Asian peasant or South Sea islander would trust himself more generally to scientific medicine. It was widely believed that the same organizational patterns and sanitary practices could be applied to other diseases. In the South, malaria, which was responsible for a larger fraction of sicknesses and deaths than all other diseases combined, existed side by side with hookworm. It is another anemia-producing disease and like hookworm, economically practical control measures were known to exist through simple anti-mosquito steps.

After five years of expanding effort in the South, the campaign was extended across the globe. The same pattern was followed with tuberculosis and then with yellow fever. The ultimate goal was not any one disease but a worldwide campaign for preventive medicine through official agencies, full-time professional staff, and modern facilities. It was the modern machinery for administering sanitary and medical care that would count, along with the awakening of public consciousness.

The task was to build up local and regional health agencies, and in this the United States had lagged behind Great Britain and Germany. Where agencies existed, they lacked funds for their work and functioned, if at all, only in times of epidemics. The technique used to strengthen county health organizations was pump priming—$2,500 a year from the external agency, with assurances that at the end of at most three years the county would take over. In Puerto Rico, Brazil, and the Philippines, it was the *municipio,* in Austria the *bezirke,* and in France the *département.* All told, the IHD appropriated more than $4 million for this purpose and today the organizational pattern for rural health services, while still needing improvement, is firmly established in many places. At the state and national levels in more than forty countries in Europe, Asia, and Latin America, a similar scheme was pursued. "Vital statistics in Colombia, public health laboratories in Costa Rica and the Philippines, a hygienic institute in Hungary, a statistical bureau in Bulgaria, a laboratory in Peking—these are random samples of the sweep and scope of the work."[6] The seeds of eventual international cooperation were planted in countries that hopefully may someday reach out to work together across ideological lines.

If ever there were a private venture in which scientific objectives were matched up with an institution's international outreach, it was the yellow fever program of the International Health Division. The story is full of personal bravery and human tragedy. Six scientists lost their lives in the search for a "solution" and on no disease up to then had a private agency placed greater emphasis or

---

[6] Raymond B. Fosdick, *The Story of The Rockefeller Foundation* (New York: Harper & Brothers, 1952), p. 40.

a larger proportion of time and financial resources. Slow progress had been made until Major Walter Reed of the United States Army Commission demonstrated in Cuba, at the time of the Spanish-American War, that yellow fever is transmitted by the mosquito *aëdes aegypti,* and not by human carriers or contaminated objects. General W. C. Gorgas, the Chief Sanitary Officer of the U.S. Army in Cuba, seized on this discovery and "eradicated" yellow fever from Havana. Three years later he extended his success in Panama, making possible the building of the Panama Canal. This led Gorgas to prophesy that yellow fever could be "eradicated from the face of the earth within a reasonable time and at reasonable cost," but this approach rested on two assumptions: (1) the *aegypti* mosquito is the sole carrier; breeds almost entirely in urban areas as distinct from the malaria mosquito which is found in swamps, rivers, and lakes; and carries infection through the man-mosquito-man cycle; and (2) key endemic centers such as Guayaquil in Ecuador are seedbeds of infection and the only source of epidemics. Both assumptions proved faulty and the epidemiology infinitely more complex.

A decade later, when the disease seemed under control if not eradicated, it struck back with savage fury. It was discovered then that yellow fever can occur in areas where there are no *aegypti* mosquitoes and that there are other carriers. It was also found, in opposition to the endemic center idea, that a form of yellow fever which existed in tropical forests in South America and Africa was the same as the disease carried by *aegypti* mosquitoes in

31

urban centers. Thus it was not enough to destroy a few endemic urban seedbeds and assume this meant the end of yellow fever. But this was knowledge that could not have been obtained through anything less than an international inquiry. Peru and Brazil in South America; Honduras, El Salvador, and Nicaragua in Central America; Mexico; and West Africa each in turn were the scenes of fateful epidemics and became therefore essential areas for research.

It proved possible to bring together in the laboratories of the Rockefeller Institute for Medical Research in New York the yellow fever viruses of Africa and Latin America and make cross immunity tests in monkeys which lead to the development of a vaccine. By the end of 1938, 1,040,000 people in Brazil and Colombia had been vaccinated and more than 90 percent developed immunity. British and American soldiers in World War II were protected in Africa and Latin America by this vaccine.

Practically all the vaccine produced since 1937, by private and public agencies, derives from an original strain of virus taken in 1927 from a West African native, Asibi, who had yellow fever. The rhesus monkey from India which was inoculated with Asibi's blood specimen died, but Asibi lived and the virus taken from him has been carried down to the present day from one laboratory animal to another through repeated multiplications and tissue cultures, affording immunity to millions of people. The blood of a single West African has served the whole human race. Because the worldwide attack on yellow fever was sustained over three decades, the disease has been pushed back into a secondary position. It remains capable of erupting in violent epidemics, but present techniques appear capable of bringing it under control. The world is the laboratory in which the control was achieved and Asibi is the human symbol of the host of mankind who contributed.

It is significant that the sites of medical and scientific work conducted by the IHD on other diseases dramatize their worldwide distribution. Rumania was the principal site for field study on scarlet fever; Puerto Rico for anemia; Tennessee for amoebic dysentery; Peru for oroya fever; Johns Hopkins for syphilis; France for undulant fever; Polynesia and Micronesia for dengue fever; and Mexico, Canada, England, France, Spain, and the United States for nutritional studies. Disease, as science, knows no nationality nor boundaries.

Malaria, which has been the major health problem of a large proportion of mankind, was the third major area in which the IHD worked. Before a demonstration of malaria control could be undertaken intelligently, the insect vectors had to be identified and the biology of each species investigated. It became clear that methods and techniques applicable in one world region could not readily be transferred to another region and sometimes not even to a different region within the same country. More importantly, *anopheles gambiae,* a carrier of a particularly severe type of malaria previously unknown in the Western Hemisphere, had in 1930 made its way from Africa to Brazil, thanks to modern means of transportation. If the argument for confining scientific activity to local diseases had merit before the era of fast destroyers and airplanes, it lost it at that point. Intercontinental and international travel necessitates international science. In 1930 and 1931 an outbreak of malaria occurred near Natal, and by 1931 *gambiae* mosquitoes had traveled 115 miles up the coast, following prevailing winds and penetrating the flat alluvial shelf at a rate of about forty miles a year. One valley had fifty thousand cases. For some districts 90 percent of the population was affected, with up to 10 percent mortality. Consternation spread, not alone in Brazil but throughout Latin and North America. The risks were described as more ominous than the penetration of yellow fever into the Far East.

In 1938 the Brazilian Health Service and Rockefeller Foundation staffs moved into North Brazil, the former with over two thousand doctors, technicians, and laborers, the latter with key organizing scientists who brought skills and resources. While this combined group, through field personnel, distributed quinine and atebrin, its major purpose was to draw a circle around the location of the *gambiae* and try to exterminate it there. The assumption was that if the *gambiae* broke through to the Parnakyba and São Francisco river valleys, its spread through the rest of South, Central, and perhaps North America could not be resisted. The *gambiae* had by then advanced halfway to the Parnakyba from Natal, spread over 300 miles, and were infesting an area of 12,000 square miles.

At first climate and geography were allies of the *gambiae,* which breeds in shallow pools of rainwater and thrives in rainy seasons. But a highly organized campaign

34

with fumigation outposts for cars and trains entering or leaving the area, a maritime service which disinfected every boat or plane bound for clean ports and a "scorched earth policy" of spreading substances like Paris green over the ground ten miles beyond the mosquitoes' advance turned back the enemy and a spreading malaria epidemic. The campaign involved an immense effort, cost $2 million but saved the Western Hemisphere.

The story of malaria dramatizes the problem of a tightly interdependent world and of the flight of carriers of disease and death from one continent to another thanks to modern aircraft and ships. Three years after the 1939–40 threat in Brazil, another invasion of Natal by *gambiae* from Accra and Dakar occurred, and Brazilian authorities again acted to turn back the threat. The lessons of these events made it plain that a spray-gun campaign at airports would never suffice—scientists must carry the war to the sources and sites of infestation in West Africa. In 1944, Egypt called for help as the *gambiae* moved north through the Nile Valley, killing 135,000 people. Once more, Foundation staff under Dr. Fred Soper and thousands of Egyptian Ministry of Health personnel met the challenge and stamped out the *gambiae*. With malaria there can be no test of success short of exterminating the last pair of the disease-carrying mosquitoes within the area concerned.

The story is not complete unless some mention is made of the most serious bottleneck of all, namely the lack of trained manpower. It soon was evident that ordinary physicians were not necessarily qualified as public health officers. It was decided to create an autonomous school of public health with an institute of hygiene at its center and closely affiliated with a medical school— a "West Point of public health." To this end, the Rockefeller Foundation built and endowed the School of Hygiene and Public Health at Johns Hopkins and subsequently supported the London School of Tropical Medicine and the Pasteur Institute in Paris. Thereafter schools and institutes of public health were developed in Prague, Warsaw, London, Toronto, Copenhagen, Budapest, Oslo, Belgrade, Zagreb, Madrid, Cluj, Ankara, Sofia, Rome, Tokyo, Athens, Bucharest, Stockholm, Calcutta, Manila, São Paulo and at the University of Michigan. More than $25 million went into this monumental effort with consequences for public health that are incalculable.

The first large-scale Foundation fellowship program was launched in health, to be followed in other fields, and from nearly every country in the world promising young students, scrupulously chosen and with assurance of scientific appointments on their return, came to the new public health institutions. Other men, already trained as public health officers, were given refresher or postgraduate courses. The aim was to link the needs in the field with powerful advanced educational centers and foster an enriching interchange of knowledge and experience. The fellowship program—an investment in leadership—gave a model that was to be followed in almost every sphere of the Foundation's work. It would be difficult to match its importance with any other social or scientific invention in the private sector.

36

All told, from 1913 to 1950, the Foundation allocated $100 million to health activities, including the awarding of 2,566 fellowships. The operating costs of field staff and offices totaled $22 million, and $8 million was appropriated for state and local health services. A total of $22 million was spent on the control and investigation of specific diseases, including $8 million for yellow fever, $4.5 million for malaria, $3.8 million for hookworm and $3 million for tuberculosis. For a private organization in the first half of the twentieth century the figures are staggering; but in response to this pump priming, the cooperating governments spent far more. The total field personnel of the IHD through its history numbered more than four hundred public health physicians, nurses, engineers, bacteriologists and others—again a mere handful in comparison with the thousands with whom they worked. Few men have won the affection and respect of as many foreign peoples or been trusted more fully. It is a classic story of partnership.

The single most important lesson to be drawn from the work of the International Health Division on specific diseases is that acquiring experience and developing machinery for an attack on specific diseases has a cumulative and aggregating effect. Momentum is built up and professional competence gained. The most natural question for the scientific body is: What disease problems should now receive our attention? For an international foundation, the worldwide character and epidemiological relationship of a disease provides one set of guidelines. The other is set by its overall priorities in programming and its estimate of urgent needs.

37

Still another consideration has importance and for private agencies can be determining. It is the presence or absence of massive competing resources that are being directed to particular needs. The original position of the IHD and its predecessor boards was an isolated and lonely one. It crossed paths with few organizations with a similarly broad and comprehensive mandate. To be sure, there was some degree of contact with the Health Organization of the League of Nations, but its field operations were limited. As time went on, private and public bodies entered the world arena with resources dwarfing those of private bodies. The Pan American Sanitary Bureau, covering twenty-one Latin American republics, had been organized in 1902 and reorganized in 1947. Its major activities included epidemic disease control, improved national health services, and public health education. By the 1950's, its annual budget was $1.9 million. The Institute of Inter-American Affairs created in 1942 devoted a part of its budget of $6 million to health and sanitation. The World Health Organization, with a basic budget of $6.15 million, provided technical experts, awarded fellowships and travel grants and undertook demonstrations and field studies. UNICEF had funds which varied from year to year depending on contributions, but in the period 1946–50, its total funds were $150 million, part of which went to WHO activities. U.S. foreign aid included funds for health and education, and the Colombo Plan funds exceeded $5 million. The United States Public Health Service represented the American government in international health relations and selected fellows and foreign service personnel. Finally, new funds entered the field from other U.S. agencies, which came to exceed those of all other bodies.

Faced with the introduction of these massive new resources and the addition of new areas of interest within the Rockefeller Foundation, such as medical education and public health, the IHD more and more turned to the clarification of basic principles rather than the application and demonstration of tried and tested technologies. It shared its knowledge with others and assigned personnel to other and newer bodies. The IHD lives on in a smaller and reorganized Foundation program and in new scientific adventures continuing to the present day, most notably the international program in virus research.

The enduring contribution of the IHD was the structure it evolved, the professionals it attracted and the goals it pursued. For a brief but critical period in the long history of man it played a solitary role, demonstrating what an international health activity under private auspices could accomplish. It left footprints that have guided others and a rich legacy that proved what can be done through people working together and through generating resources from the private sector. There can be little doubt that currently urgent activities in population control and health care draw working models from this respected and pioneering body.

Yet the new areas run the risk of being more politicized than professionalized or they reflect the noble impulses and energies of a few powerful and fanatical reformers. These impulses, however worthy, are mixed with an immense amount of selfish pride and desire for personal advancement and sometimes are oblivious to the need for instruments such as the IHD. Or when the instruments exist, they are not always wisely and fully used. To the extent reformers leave to scientists the shaping of scientific decisions, the more likely they are to carve out in history a place comparable to that of the IHD. The quite modest advances that have been made thus far in a field like population underscore this warning. The same need for clarity of objectives and sharpness of instruments exists in these complex fields as it did five decades ago in health. It is instructive therefore to review and reexamine this earliest chapter in private foreign assistance.

# 3: CONCEPTS AND PRECEPTS IN EDUCATIONAL AND SCIENTIFIC COOPERATION

If we turn to the wider area of international cooperation in education and science, it is clear that forces are at work today that threaten the historic role of the United States as an initiator and leader. Some are a part of the fabric of the total national and international scene and are not unique to educational relations. They include the pressures of urgent domestic needs, the incipient neo-isolationism born of weariness and Vietnam, a crisis of confidence over foreign aid among liberals and conservatives alike, and a dawning consciousness that all the well-advertised strategies for building solidarity in the world have failed to usher in the millenium. We are hard put to locate our moment in history. Perhaps it is the morning after and the nation is pausing to measure and balance its interest, capacities, and commitments vis-à-vis the rest of the world. However, anxieties and emotions unleashed in recent times make us fear that we are precariously balanced on the threshold of a fateful era of retreat and withdrawal, marking a loss of the sense of direction and self-confidence required of a world leader.

41

Who can say if this republic, as others before it, has lost the heart and will to be a world leader? It is not for either pessimists or optimists—who would speak prematurely for us and for generations yet unborn—but for history to mold the answer to this awesome question.

The future shape of educational and scientific relations is linked in a narrower sense with trends and experiences extending over three-quarters of a century. This is true of the broad area of international educational exchange. For more than fifty years, educators and intellectuals assumed they were serving the cause of world unity and furthering the growth of trained leaders by one-way educational exchange seen as an unqualified good. Sound educational objectives and missionary impulses merged in inspiring Americans to bring young people one by one or to airlift them by scores to educational centers here. Hundreds and even thousands more in every field and at every stage of educational advancement have found their separate ways to American institutions, until in the sixties the total enrolled approached 125,000 annually.

Positive as this approach has been in many respects, it suffers from serious defects. There is often a lack of prior planning, selection processes have been hastily thrown up, carefully developed study plans linking home institutions with centers abroad have been lacking, and uncertainty about positions to which the students could return has haunted their future. Most serious, however, has been the failure to articulate training here with institution building in the developing countries. Consequently, the emphasis today is shifting more and more to a two-way traffic, with American professionals joining as partners in building strong and relevant centers in Africa, Asia, Latin America, and the Middle East, while reserving study opportunities in American universities for graduate and professional training. This two-way traffic has increasingly been viewed as part of a single process aimed at concurrently searching out promising individuals and institutional frameworks within which their future growth and continuing responsibility would be possible. Visiting American professors, who add new-found loyalties to the developing institution to ongoing commitments at U.S. universities, serve as a bridge in assisting these younger scholars.

This major shift in the theory and practice of this form of international educational relations has its roots in changing values and objectives, which must be thoroughly reviewed and studied to determine the national and international context of such relations. Unless this changing context is more fully grasped and understood, the noble intentions that inspire international exchanges will lead as often to crippling as to constructive results, breed misunderstanding, and undermine worldwide confidence in cultural relations.

The student of international cooperation, if he probes the context of international educational relations, will discover forces at work that can best be stated in dichotomies. These include: the need for international cooperation to solve common problems vs. the need to develop national self-confidence for creative solutions to

43

national problems; technological advance vs. ecological balance; efficient development through centralization of power vs. popular participation and the generating of individual initiative through decentralization; and the emergence of new values appropriate to modernization vs. the preservation of traditional values. Each of these dichotomies merits more extended study, but the points of tension and conflict are obvious.

Few would question the need for international cooperation to solve common problems. Infinite threads of human need bind all men together. Science knows no national boundaries where hunger and famine, the spread of pestilence and disease, or the movement of plagues and blights that threaten plant and animal life (as with wheat rust or infectious diseases) are concerned. As the problems threatening mankind are international, their alleviation requires the sharing of knowledge on an international basis. In Raymond Fosdick's memorable phrase: "In peace as in war we are all of us the beneficiaries of contributions to knowledge made by every nation in the world."[1]

At the same time, newly independent states suddenly thrust into the maelstrom of an uncertain world must develop national self-confidence in order to adapt tradition creatively to meet new problems. New governments must demonstrate they are capable of serving their own people. International cooperation may bring into play

[1] *The Rockefeller Foundation Annual Report*—1941, President's Review, p. 10.

dependency relationships with accompanying obstacles to national self-determination. Thus a potential tension exists between international cooperation and national development—and those who administer educational and scientific relations must be sensitive to this.

Particularly in the developing countries the appropriation of knowledge and of technological advances is crucial to building modern societies—yet this occurs at a time when the human and ecological costs of industrialization are ever more apparent. The urgency of achieving greater ecological balance within developed societies opens up broad new areas for discovering common interests essential to improved cultural relations. Yet new nations must never feel that talk about ecology is a way for the rich to deny the fruits of progress to the poor. Industrialization must be pursued along with the search for ecological balance.

Modernization, which has become a primary objective of the developing states, historically has required centralization. From the time of the industrial revolution, the concentration at one point of efforts in both private and public sectors has been the precondition for industrial and agricultural advancement, increasing national incomes, generating capital, and assuring economic growth. Once again, the developing nations sense a changing emphasis in the more developed nations, with new stress on decentralization, the creation of multiple centers of economic and political decision-making, and new forms of revenue sharing. A partnership for devel-

45

opment, therefore, calls for a sensitive awareness of the need for progress along all fronts.

Similarly, in this country changing life styles, the growing role of minorities in forming national attitudes, and the reestablishment of semirural patterns of living in suburbs and in communal groupings throw into question the worldwide trend toward urbanization and modernization which has supplanted the traditions and values of Jefferson and Thoreau. Modern American culture and counter-culture exist side by side, and only the most daring of our prophets presume to foresee the outcome or anticipate the survival of these competing trends. Few are sanguine enough in their prescience to select out the social and cultural patterns likely to persist by the year 2000.

Therefore, the point to be made in considering the nation's cultural context, in relation to which international educational and scientific relations work themselves out, is that once firmly rooted factors are in flux. Contending forces are at work which make up the raw stuff in "a great debate" about international educational and scientific relations and "the societies men seek." If the developed societies were ever able to offer simple development blueprints to the rest of the world, this time has passed. Four areas at least require further study and analysis. In this study, the annals of private foreign assistance may illuminate the problems involved in:

1. Ways to manage society and translate this experience in terms that are operationally relevant to others;

2. Ways to develop a critical mass of talent, nation-

ally and internationally, in certain areas identified as of special importance;

3. Ways to help ourselves and others in creating a non-xenophobic sense of nationalism to facilitate the growth of integrative and unifying processes within nations, alongside developing cosmopolitanism; and

4. Reevaluation of the contributions which individual societies can make to each other as they draw on the special competence and unique resources that others can offer. Each society has the task of identifying its areas of particular strength and its needs. As the level of development increases, so does interdependence and the need for international cooperation.

The private sector has had a reasonable amount of experience in joining with friends abroad in operationally relevant enterprises. The "operating programs," so-called, of the private foundations are one example of partnership in the building of relevant structures directed to urgent national needs. The Ford Foundation has pioneered in working with the economic planning agencies of governments in the developing countries. The International Health Division of the Rockefeller Foundation was first in the field in assistance to Ministries of Health and, beginning in 1943, the cooperative agricultural programs of the same Foundation have worked with Ministries of Agriculture.

If these experiences point up any lessons concerning cooperation in the management of vital domestic sectors of proud and intensely nationalistic regimes, the first lesson is that those who would serve must operate within the "system." It will not do to set up alternative structures wholly outside the system, for governments requiring popular support can ill afford to share prestige and credit with aliens or other groups. I recall a discussion with Julius Nyerere antedating the independence of Tanganyika. In evaluating the need for external assistance in education, this forceful leader, destined to become his nation's chief executive, expressed strong preference for help in higher rather than elementary education. No government dependent on public support, he said, could afford to face the electorate without having proven its capacity on its own to establish and maintain public education for the great mass of young people as far as secondary school. Moreover, this problem is in no sense restricted to education. A similar reticence expressed itself in the Philippines, where every international agency but one was spoken of in single word acronyms: Fao (the Food and Agriculture Organization), Who (the World Health Organization), and Uno (the United Nations Organization). However, Philippine leaders, perhaps for political and psychological reasons even they did not fully comprehend, could never bring themselves to use the word *Aid* for the Agency for International Development. The stigma and trauma of dependency was too great. While private agencies may suppose their help can be kept free of political reactions, experience has shown that anxiety is always present, oftentimes just below the surface.

Sensitivity, which pervades and surrounds every cooperative international effort, is doubtless most acute with public national or international agencies. Examples drawn from the private sector of technical assistance suggest that in certain cases the representatives of private agencies enjoy a comparative advantage. Visiting scientists who serve under the banner of private agencies with long-established international programs are less often tarred with an imperialist brush. For example, the government of the People's Republic of China renamed Peking Union Medical College, to which the Rockefeller Foundation had given $40 million before World War II, the Anti-Imperialist Medical Center, and most recently, the Capital Hospital. But the early medical scientists who served there were respected and honored as individuals in China, and who can say what influence their legacy may have as we enter the new era in Sino-American relations.

In a similar way in other lands, a path has been cleared for visiting scientists by predecessors who earned trust and respect by long years of dedicated service. Theirs is a legacy of devotion to the well-being of mankind across national and ideological boundaries. It would be an exaggeration to claim that they can enjoy immunity from criticism in highly charged political environments, but it is historically true that they often are the last to feel the hammer blows of nationalist criticism.

The history of American foundations' activity abroad also throws light on the possibilities and problems of developing a critical mass of talent nationally and internationally in fields of special importance. The Achilles heel of most international programs is people, pure and

49

simple. The task of developing sectors of strength within developing societies is too exacting and complex to be left to "marginal men." The leaders of the developing nations not infrequently call for our best. Our Indian friends, for example, characteristically ask for the best scholars and scientists in the developed nations—pre-eminent educational leaders recognized worldwide for their scientific credentials. Leaders of this stamp are seldom attracted by projects of limited life expectancy. However short-term their own commitment may be, such scientists ask assurance that the enterprise to which they assign precious months and years of their all too brief professional careers has long-term prospects. The prerequisites for long life include a serious commitment by the cooperating American institution and its ruling body, which for a major foundation is its board of trustees, to see the job through with good prospects for continued financing. They also include the continued functioning of a nucleus of fully qualified visiting professionals able to meet the challenges that lie ahead. Here again foundations, which can limit the scope of their efforts and possess long-standing ties with centers of professional competence in the educationally advanced societies, have a comparative advantage in attracting and holding first-class professionals. The heart of their effort is the concept of a career service and the records of the operating foundations are intimately bound up with the efforts of long-term professionalism.

Similarly, the annals of foundation experience are illustrative of the dynamics of nation-building through educational channels. Freed of the need to publicize for annual congressional hearings what Americans abroad have achieved in the national interest, soundly based foundation programs can redound predominantly to the benefit of recipient nations. There is less need to stamp "made in the United States" on each and every human and material contribution. The stakes are long-term, as are the careers of those responsible; for them proof and credit are less pressing in the short term. It is significant that Norman Borlaug, Rockefeller Foundation agricultural scientist in Mexico, had worked for nearly three decades on wheat before he received the Nobel Prize.

This is not to suggest that private foundations are unresponsive to the broad outlines of public policy or indifferent to the national interest. No foundation would embark on a program in another nation if it were directly contrary to public policy in its own country. Actions are not taken in the face of sharply drawn governmental strictures against working in particular countries. Once a decision has been made within the framework of accepted national policy, however, to embark on a serious program, the flexibility and freedom to define working objectives and carry them through in accordance with well-tested foundation procedures is an immensely valuable asset. It is possible for foundation staff to operate "with a passion for anonymity" in the country they freely choose to serve. Military and strategic considerations don't directly intrude. Political assessments of worth need not threaten continued service. Most basic to any lasting contribution is freedom to transfer, easily and unhesitat-

51

ingly, the credit for each advance to the local personnel with whom scientists work. Nothing is as likely to facilitate the growth of the integrative and unifying processes within the new nations as this controlling precept of private foreign assistance.

In a fourth area, foundation programs can be carried forward on the basis of mutuality of interest and resources. The first step, which precedes the decision to join in a cooperative venture, is a firm and unequivocal invitation from the nation seeking assistance. A working agreement involves commitments on both sides. The best test of the importance which a recipient government or institution attaches to a program is its willingness to commit national resources. Mutuality can also be measured against a government's willingness to accord privileges and immunities to foreign scientists working in their midst. If equipment and materials given for scientific purposes are taxed or held back, a shadow is thrown on the seriousness of intent and purpose of those seeking help. A nation entering into a cooperative program must see it as "a partnership in all things." Its response is an earnest of an underlying conviction that it too has a role to play in building mutuality of interest.

Finally, it is essential that participants in foreign assistance try to foresee the kind of intellectual leadership the world will require ten, twenty, or thirty years from now—the kind and size of the most urgent emerging problems with which all leaders must be equipped to contend. Those who write on international cooperation, while recognizing the priority that must be given to immediately pressing problems, have prophesied that ten or twenty years from now the differences between rich and poor, developed and underdeveloped societies will become submerged in other more narrowly definable problems such as the social and ecological effects of technology, jobs and employment, population increase, fiscal balance, and education. The international consequences of these problems are outrunning adaptations in present structures. It seems clear that for the developing countries, access to the international system of technology and an ability to cope with ecological concerns will be more important than the sheer volume of financial aid they receive. It is not enough for Americans to focus on the definition of future problems. They must also consider the role which American experience and expectations can play in furthering understanding of the problems. To make it possible to proceed from identification to the solution of these problems, there must be changes here and throughout the world in attitudes of national leaders and of the general public.

## A CENTRAL FOCUS ON LEADERSHIP

Leadership is the instrumentality through which men and nations cope with immediate, intermediate, and long-range problems, and in foreign assistance it is imperative to focus on the identification, training, and uses of leadership. The task of national leaders is to define, from within the particular context of each nation and society, those goals and purposes toward which national energy and resources must be directed. They must be enabled to fight for the realization of those broad purposes. It is futile to try to make a society want to realize goals identified by outsiders. At the same time, every society needs information and skills which can be employed to achieve dominant aims and purposes. Assistance in developing these skills is likely the most fruitful area for intercultural relations.

A writer and adviser to universities, foundations, and American industry has suggested that two broad categories of leadership are essential for institutions in every society, developed and developing: "operators" and "conceptualizers." The "operator" is the leader who has:

> the ability to carry the enterprise toward its objectives, in the situation, from day-to-day, and resolve the issues that arise as this movement takes place. This calls for interpersonal skills, sensitivity to the immediate environment, tenacity, experience, judgment, ethical soundness, and related attributes and abilities. . . .[2]

A "conceptualizer" on the other hand, has:

> the ability to see the whole in the perspective of history —past and future—to state and adjust goals, to evaluate, to analyze, and to foresee contingencies a long way ahead. Long-range strategic planning is embraced here, as is setting standards and judging performance. Leadership, in the sense of going out ahead to show the way, is more conceptual than operating. *Conceptual* . . . is not synonymous with "intellectual" or "theoretical."

[2] Robert K. Greenleaf in an unpublished memorandum made available to the author.

The conceptualizer, at his best, is a persuader and a relations-builder.[3]

The great problem of institutions everywhere, as they develop cadres of leadership, is to maintain the right blend of conceptualizers and operators. It is true that conceptualizers are generally lacking in qualities required of the operator. Under most circumstances, however, operators tend to drive out conceptualizers. Usually conceptualizers, perhaps from a sense of insecurity about their ability to handle delicate personal relations, are aware of the need for operators and are good at setting standards for operators to follow. However, if an operator rises to the top of a large institution, he oftentimes fails to see the need for conceptualizers because he has difficulty in visualizing what they contribute. Within most structures, conceptualizers have to be organized into groups large enough to protect themselves. The two most important steps in the selection and use of conceptualizers are, first, the decision that institutions need conceptualizers and, second, the creating of an environment in which their contributions and talents can be used and maintained.

The idea of conceptualizers joined together in a kind of mutual protection society has special relevance to international cooperation. Once an area of need is identified, a case can be made for training scholars abroad, not as isolated individuals but in sufficient numbers so that they will constitute a critical mass on returning home. In most nations and international organizations today there is a

[3] *Ibid.*

desperate need for new ideas that can shake people and organizations free from outmoded concepts and procedures. The operator is inclined to say "why give up a winning horse!" A new generation of conceptualizers will be needed once the present operators recognize the need for new ideas. New institutional forms can seldom be imported wholesale without adaptations, but both conceptualizers and operators with the requisite inherent and acquired skills will be needed to choose, adapt, and implement according to the needs of the individual society. It is obvious that everyone is part conceptualizer and part operator and that these talents need not exist in isolation. The two types of leadership are ideal types. The task is to assure that those who have one or the other of such talents in abundance are utilized to the full and allowed to flower and grow. Leadership and its various forms and combinations runs like a red thread through every successful experiment in intercultural relations.

The most enduring contribution of the private sector may well prove to be its fellowship and scholarship programs, which basically are nothing more than leadership development. It would be difficult to show that the over ten thousand fellowship and scholarship awards of the Rockefeller Foundation from 1917 to 1970 were matched by any other endeavor in its history. Surely no comparable effort in foreign assistance can match the number of Nobel laureates proportionate to fellowships awarded in the roster of European biomedical, natural science, and economics fellowships. The present leadership in Asian, African, and Latin American universities is a further index to the quality of this enterprise, and we can expect equally great things from them.

Yet it would be difficult to imagine a record of this type emerging from larger, less flexible, or more diffuse undertakings in leadership development. The prerequisites assume continuing trust and support by those who authorize expenditures for fellowship awards. They require a rigorous and unflagging pursuit of excellence within a carefully defined sphere of activity. The selection process must be based on criteria and standards evolved over time. Professionals must choose would-be professionals, with due attention to the cultural context within which the returning scholar must operate. The granting agency must have the staff to choose wisely, administer efficiently, and retain contact throughout the study period. Above all, those who would help must be flexible and keep ever in mind that "the school of a scholar" in a foreign assistance effort is subject to all the intangibles and vagaries that go with living and working abroad. For some scholars the pursuit of a degree may proceed like clockwork, while for others language difficulties, family complications, or lack of preparation may delay the process. There is nothing automatic or mechanical about earning an advanced degree and the first law for the fellowship administrator should be: "Be ye as flexible as you would have others be."

Foundations with professional staffs are geared to individual efforts and to the needs of the fledgling educator. They can "bet" on the exceptional individual, controversial though he may be, trust and assist him in his training, help him develop a study plan tailored to his needs and opportunity, communicate with universities at home and abroad which have a stake in his future, and stand by him through successes and failures. In the end, some aspiring academic or research leaders may fail, but the time-worn adage from baseball should serve as a motto for those who give assistance: "A .333 batting average often wins the crown." Any scheme for helping promising individuals is a risky business and only an agency with risk capital should enter the lists. The rewards in having a modest part in the career development of a unique individual outweigh the risks.

If those who hold in trust the use of private funds did nothing else but multiply future leaders for the developing countries, they would deserve the privileged status accorded them by law and public policy. In this regard, responsible American leaders at work in this sphere of international cooperation express concern about a "cloud on the horizon no larger than a man's hand." In mass societies with pressures to deal in aggregates and numbers, the problems of highly individualized programs multiply and are more difficult to sustain. The staff time required to select highly promising individuals is as great as that of making choices for institutional support. Paper work mushrooms and administrative guidance and counseling is more, not less, exacting. More seriously, hard-pressed graduate schools in the United States and elsewhere, given expanding national enrollments, find there are fewer places open for students from other lands. Questions are raised about hidden costs and inquiries concerning supplementary payments are increasingly directed to private foundations. Most serious of all, however, is the uncertainty which prevails regarding the taxable income of fellowship students whose stipends are provided by American foundations. If an increasingly larger proportion of fellowship awards are made subject to tax withholding, fewer awards can be given and a smaller number of leaders will be trained. Add to this the declining value of the same number of dollars and we come full circle.

Thus a case can be made for reexamining the implications of recent trends. Private organizations must and do operate within the framework of national policy. The question that must be asked is whether or not it is in the national interest that qualified scientists and educators from countries around the world be trained promptly and effectively by American institutions. If the answer to such a question is affirmative, then it would seem that public policy should be formulated to facilitate and not impede this purpose. For it remains as true today as has always been the case that every successful venture in international cooperation presupposes qualified leadership. When economists speak of a nation's infrastructure as the necessary precondition for the successful use of capital assistance, they mean roads and harbors, public administration and institutional development in the recipient country. But more fundamentally still, they refer to trained manpower and human skills, without which productive use of assistance is impossible.

The single most dramatic example of successful international cooperation since World War II has been the

Marshall Plan. Its success can be traced to the existence in Western Europe of large reservoirs of so-called human capital—trained and skilled personnel able to organize and administer programs. When Americans turned their attention to the less-developed parts of the world, it was at first assumed that a model was ready and at hand in the Marshall Plan. The early history of Point Four proved the analogy did not hold. Belatedly, we discovered that lacking trained leaders (on its independence from Belgium, Zaïre had seven college graduates among its nationals), assistance programs floundered. The indigenous resources were not at hand for the management and planning of programs.

Thus international cooperation is dependent on people willing and able to use both national and external resources. The *sine qua non* is trained manpower. It is therefore inconceivable that Americans could be in favor of international cooperation and opposed, whether by intent or indifference, to the preparation of well-qualified leaders from abroad.

# 4: A SUCCESS STORY IN INTERNATIONAL COOPERATION:
## LEADERSHIP AND PARTNERSHIP IN AGRICULTURE

In an era of profound social change, when all aspects of national and international life are under scrutiny and review, it is vital that successes and failures in international scientific and educational relations be examined. The most dramatic success story in recent times may be the cooperative programs in agriculture that have led to "the green revolution." The history of this remarkable effort can be measured against the criteria of the development of cooperative solutions to urgent "human species problems" and of building indigenous capacity through the training of leaders. If it is true that the core of international cultural relations is the purposeful exchange of knowledge and skills, especially knowledge and skills which can be used toward solving problems which affect the entire world, agricultural programs can also be measured against this standard.

The three questions worth raising for every form of international cooperation are: (1) Is there a clear, evident, and identifiable problem mutually put forward by partners in international cooperation as a priority need? (2) Is there consensus deriving from a singularity of purpose that knowledge and skills sharply focused and sustained will result in solutions to a problem? (3) Is there intercultural receptivity based upon the recognition that local skills are lacking, external assistance is needed, and the values of cooperation will outweigh socially disruptive consequences? Scientific cooperation provides particularly dramatic examples, most recently that of "the green revolution," in which all three questions can be answered in the affirmative. It has yet to be proven that this is true of social problems in which consensus is more difficult to achieve. At the same time, the lack of dramatic success stories in social fields hardly justifies failure to join in a focused and sustained attack on clearly identifiable social problems, as, for example, the unemployment issue.

The international agricultural program initiated by the Rockefeller Foundation, and vigorously supported for a decade or more by the Ford Foundation and others, can be ranked as a success story of major proportions in the transfer of knowledge and skills. It is possible to study this striking cooperative enterprise in terms of its underlying concepts and principles; the stages, processes and methods employed; organization and institutionalization; the development and sustaining of leadership; the consequences of successes and failures; transferability of lessons learned; and some of the unsolved problems and unfinished business.

The "father" of the cooperative Mexican Agricultural Program of the Rockefeller Foundation and the retiring Foundation president, Dr. J. George Harrar, sees the human side of the effort as involving cultural relations in the most fundamental terms. From the outset there was interplay among a wide variety of individuals. The lesson of the fieldwork approach, in which participation involved a broad segment of rural and governmental life, is that leadership potential exists in amazing array, however latent, and through nurture and guidance can be made to flower. In 1941 the Foundation was invited by the government of Mexico to join in helping to solve a clear, identifiable, and priority problem, the severe crop deficit in corn, wheat, and beans. The yields were already too low to satisfy the demands of a nation of 16 million people, and population was growing rapidly. The need was self-evident and pressing; Mexico was obliged to use scarce foreign exchange to import corn and wheat, detracting from possibilities for genuine economic growth. The Mexicans lacked the trained personnel and the know-how to solve the problem, but they had confidence that working with the Rockefeller Foundation they would find answers. Inspired by a singular purpose, the government of Mexico and its future leaders sat down with Foundation leaders to define the various facets of the problem, map out priorities, and commit national resources to match the efforts of the Foundation.

If the need was clear, the detailed steps for meeting it were not. The Foundation sent a three-man survey team which traveled extensively, examined the way crops were grown, and learned all that could be learned about the situation. By 1943, their survey established the fact that in wheat, the Mexican varieties then in use were low-yielding, genetically impure and subject to wheat rust. Practically all the existing varieties had to be grown in irrigated areas. In areas where there was rain, fungus grew and the wheat died. This left much of the available land unused and irrigation was not available for other crops when needed. Similar problems existed in both corn and beans. This defined the problem, and Mexicans and Americans set out to discover the elements making up "a solution."

The informing principle of the program from the start was that it must be a Mexican program. Nothing would be done without the cooperation of the host country's leaders, scientists, and educators, so they could be credited with the results and accomplishments. It was located in the Ministry of Agriculture in a specially created Office of Special Studies. The successes were Mexican, as with the "Mexican wheat" recently sent to India and Pakistan, but Mexico also had to live with all the consequences. It was a partnership in good and bad days and a true experiment in international cooperation. Ultimately, the entire activity was turned over totally to the Mexicans, and now it is paid for, led, and manned wholly by Mexicans. A small research arm involving many of the same scientists is sponsored internationally today under the designation of the International Maize and Wheat Improvement Center (CIMMYT).

Thus, the stages in the development of the program were: (1) its creation and institutionalization; (2) its growth and development; (3) a period of disengagement and full Mexicanization; and (4) its internationalization.

## A Success Story in Agriculture

The success of the effort is due as much to mutual understanding between the Mexicans and those who worked with them as to anything else. Mexicans are a proud people. They have an idea about the colossus of the North which makes them suspicious, and this is, of course, understandable. Porfiro Diaz said, "Poor Mexico —so far from God and so near to the United States." Across this gulf of historic anxieties and insecurities, the leaders had to learn to communicate with one another and how to achieve the desired results. It was necessary to demonstrate how difficult things were and how they could be improved. There were those who had a vested interest in the low level of production, and one of the most sensitive problems was to make the existing inadequacies self-evident. It was necessary to associate with the program those who would otherwise have been shown up by its success and to make it a team effort. There were persistent problems and close calls, but the skill of the leadership on both sides helped to surmount them. The leadership group included both "conceptualizers" and "operators." The important thing, in Harrar's words, was to work hard and maintain a low profile. The spirit of the effort was always low-keyed.

It is fair to ask who gave impetus to the stage by stage evolution of the program. The simple answer is the Mexicans. The professional staff from the outside never exceeded ten to twelve scientists, with the larger number of administrative personnel being primarily Mexican. They proved to themselves that they were capable of accomplishing their own version of "the green revolution." This encouraged and stimulated them to extend their best efforts and to reach out to others to share in their success. For example, Mexico had been unwilling in the 1940's to share new seeds and varieties even with their closest neighbors, the Central American countries. By the 1950's Mexico was sending young scientists to help in other countries and to share new varieties, seeds, and crop practices. A Middle East wheat program was inaugurated from a Mexican base. The wheat which led to the crop breakthrough in West Pakistan was introduced there by a Mexican trained in the cooperative program. A Mexican went to India to work on potatoes and Mexicans are working in the 1970's at the International Center of Tropical Agriculture (CIAT) in Colombia. From these and other efforts, Mexico is beginning to take satisfaction and to see itself as a world leader. It has become a country with its own expertise and a conviction that technical assistance should not flow from the industrially developed countries alone. Each country has a role to play if there is to be a truly international system.

Yet it must also be said that there was a vision at the center, perhaps not always articulated but present nonetheless. A mystique surrounded the combined efforts of Mexicans and Americans. They came to believe increasingly that they were caught up in a grand alliance for the peaceful transformation of agricultural production. The key personnel on both sides put on overalls and went into the fields. Mexicans who sometimes had viewed top positions as white-collar jobs discovered that agricultural sciences meant planting a crop and orienting their day-by-day work to increased production. The restless, driving personalities of the principals permeated the whole enterprise and inspired everyone to accomplish more than they imagined possible.

The human side of the program and the intriguing interplay of personalities deserves a full-scale history prepared by those who knew it best. A few glimpses which derive from the personal accounts of men such as Harrar, Norman Borlaug, and Ed Wellhausen point to the direction this history may take. It was essential that hope be kept alive throughout early trials and tribulations. Land for experimental agricultural work and for proper field station facilities was pieced together plot by plot. Mexican officials required proof that their commitment of resources was worth the price. There were setbacks, as with the passing from the scene of individual Mexican leaders at critical stages when their cooperation might have assured accelerated progress. Certain inputs which leaders considered essential were lacking or were in short supply. Although it was recognized that work must be done to improve storage, transportation, and land use, there were limitations or delays that hampered advancement in these areas to match achievements in crop production. It may be that the highly qualified soil scientists and plant pathologists were, consciously or not, skeptical and even suspicious of the style and working habits of strange breeds of agricultural scientists, such as agricultural economists. In all events, the Mexican program was slow to build up competence in these fields.

What is impressive, however, is that many of the scientists who were to head up efforts in Colombia, Chile, the Philippines, India, and Nigeria were alumni of this first effort. What they learned and appropriated there was to prepare them for new endeavors elsewhere. Those such as Borlaug who remained in Mexico were seized with the ultimate importance of their work. Prone both to great enthusiasm and to a burdening sense of discouragement, Borlaug believed Harrar's promise that if he persisted the world would pay him tribute as someone who had changed the map of wheat production. Not only was this prophecy fulfilled, but so was the one that crop deficits could be erased and the country's economy turned around. Thanks to these humane efforts and to the mystique of possible success, the momentum was sustained from one stage to the next. A particularly vital stage in the Mexican program involved its being shifted wholly to Mexican leadership. The theory underlying this stage is that there is always a magic moment—extraordinarily difficult to identify—when transfer should take place, accompanied by gradual withdrawal into other fields of aid or other geographical areas. There must be a sense of having worked oneself out of a job. Once the job has been reasonably well begun, it is vital that it be transferred to nationals. Those from the outside must leave the front line, get in back and push.

From the beginning of the process, Rockefeller Foundation scientists associated themselves with young Mexicans who served as in-service trainees. In 1943, no one in Mexico had the equivalent of even an M.A. in agricultural sciences. The Foundation staff and Mexican trainees went into the field and worked together. They applied what they knew to the Mexican scene and drew know-how from the environment. They solved the wheat rust problem genetically by collecting germ plasm from all over the world. The farmers were encouraged to invest more in seeds and fertilizer, and yields increased from approximately 750 kg. a hectare to 3,200 kg. a hectare today. At the same time they learned from local people, for example, that you don't plant corn in a particular phase of the moon because it turned out this was the time when army ants hatched and moved through the fields. They learned you could not translate American experience wholesale but had to depend on mutual understanding of experience and goals.

In the case of corn, there was a greater variety of problems—bad management and planning, low-yielding varieties, poor nutritional values, pests, and so forth. These were corrected and a system was developed with a better package of practices plus a rational formula for using improved seeds. Germ plasm was also gathered and stored, and new hybrids sought. The pace of progress here in comparison with wheat reflected the differences within which each program had to function, but by 1948 Mexico no longer had to import corn. To reach this same point in wheat took until 1956, even though the overall progress in wheat is generally considered to have been more dramatic.

The young American scientists recruited by Dr. Harrar to serve in Mexico were not frozen into a particular scientific or disciplinary point of view. Here another principle emerged that was to have its application in other areas of Foundation programs. Men were chosen who were willing to dedicate themselves to the central task and to develop a career abroad without the recognition and dividends of working professionally in the United States. This staff became the nucleus of the Foundation and International Institutes' agricultural staffs today, much as the doctors and public-health specialists who were members of the medical staff had earlier gone on to serve in the International Health Division. The majority are still with the Foundation. Others have gone on to head departments in American universities but are still in touch with the Foundation and its work, and serve periodically in important posts at home and abroad. They were needed because there was no body of highly trained and experienced personnel. Mutual agreement and understanding on the part of the Mexican political and scientific leadership was equally essential, along with candor in describing the situation and the problems.

An important factor contributing to crop deficits was ignorance concerning available world knowledge. Thus Mexicans had not known of strains and varieties that had been developed in the United States fifteen years earlier. Now, at the international centers such as CIMMYT and IRRI (the International Rice Research Institute in the Philippines), a primary aim is to make certain that each country knows all that can be known about strains which are available in germ plasm banks and which may be adapted to serve their needs. The lessons of Mexico have been applied and their application accelerated in the international institutes partly because a model had been tested and partly because their resources are many times those with which Harrar and his colleagues had to work (his annual budget initially was $30,000, compared with $1,500,000 for the institutes today). The legacy of Mexico in this respect has spread around the world. Whether the effort is a national or international one, working principles are much the same. Approaches and solutions must be developed from clearly outlined priorities. A firm resolve must be made to stay within these priorities and to avoid scatteration and dispersion of energy. The axiom —it is more important to solve two or three things than to fail with forty—has become a first principle. There must be adequate resources to support the effort itself, but super-adequate resources can be bad. Dr. Harrar, in referring to the limited finances of the early Mexican effort, has observed it is sometimes good to be a little hungry, because it forces men to work harder in developing local resources. In his words: "It is vital to have the necessary tools, but these oftentimes are seeds and hoes, not electron microscopes."

There is another part of the legacy which is more human than scientific. A competent and able staff, including their families, can be living ambassadors for improved cultural relations. Their lives and well-being are crucial to their task, as is their happiness. They contribute most when whole families see themselves as fellow ambassadors and are proud and content with their lives abroad. Men serving in such a cause function better where the task is long-term and they operate on a career and professional basis. The question is often asked how long is long-term? They must remain as long as is necessary to make lasting contributions. The formula should not be "we will go in and solve it in three years!" But rather, "we will go in and stay until we have reached a certain goal, and we don't know how long that will take." Other programs which have had hopeful beginnings were not sustained and their positive results lost as a result. It is also worth noting that some of the earlier efforts, including those by ICA/AID, helped pave the way for others which followed, even though the first attempts never flowered as fully developed, continuing programs.

Career people must have a deep professional interest in solving a problem; their objective must be not science in general but, quite single-mindedly, that of making headway in their primary purpose: of improving rice, corn, or wheat production. They must be a cohesive group with a common objective. There is no simple distinction between short-term and long-term or pure and applied research. The only question to ask is whether the research is relevant to the problem.

Visiting scientists must double or triple in brass, for in the beginning in some developing countries there are at most a handful of qualified scientists. East Pakistan had only two government entomologists for the entire country. Initially only one scientist was assigned by the outside agencies to the crop improvement program in Thailand and one wheat expert in Pakistan. From Mexico to the present time the lesson of the cooperative agricultural programs has been that a handful of men can go a long way toward solving the food issue—if they are the right men.

Building on the lessons and accomplishments in Mexico, the Ford and Rockefeller Foundations in the 1960's joined with other private national and international agencies in creating four international institutes; in Mexico (corn and wheat); the Philippines (rice); and most recently in Nigeria and Colombia (a broad-based approach to the problems of tropical agriculture). At the International Center of Tropical Agriculture in Colombia, as in Nigeria, the focus is not on a single crop but on soil, water, and crop and livestock improvements. The mutually agreed upon problem is the inescapable fact that the tropics are among the most unproductive areas in the world, yet have the greatest potential for food production, with 365-day growing seasons, nearly unlimited land, and abundant sun and water. These areas may hold the answer to massive increases in the world's food supply even though their production today lags behind that of other areas with fewer natural advantages. The work of the two new institutes has only begun and any evaluation now would be premature. IRRI and CIMMYT have already raised production and GNP in Asia, the Middle East, and Latin America. The point to be made is that they are building on and extending the experience and principles embodied in the Mexican program.

The one international institute whose brief but dramatic history is appropriately placed alongside the Mexican success story is the International Rice Research

Institute in the Philippines. The points of similarity and difference in philosophy, origin, and development of the two experiments are instructive. In both cases, the early formative thought that led to initiatives was concentrated in a relatively few minds. The "Mexican idea" emerged in a conversation between the late Henry A. Wallace and Raymond B. Fosdick, then president of the Rockefeller Foundation. Nothing would contribute more to the welfare of Mexico and the happiness of its people, Wallace prophesied, than increasing yields in corn and beans. The "three Musketeers" appointed by President Fosdick traveled more than five thousand miles through Mexico in the summer of 1941 as members of a survey commission and were instrumental in recommending action and serving as consultants over the years. The three were E. C. Stakman, plant pathologist at the University of Minnesota; Richard Bradfield, soil scientist at Cornell University; and Paul C. Mangelsdorf, geneticist and authority on corn at Harvard University. But the major responsibility fell on a thirty-seven-year-old plant pathologist and department head at Washington State College who moved to Mexico in 1943 and was to be both resident "conceptualizer" and "operator," Dr. J. George Harrar.

The quip has been made that the grand design of the International Rice Research Institute "was conceived in Scarsdale and exported to Los Baños." If there is any truth in this colorful expression, it stems from the common residence of two of the "intellectual fathers" of IRRI. Both Dr. Harrar and Dr. F. F. Hill, Vice President for International Programs at the Ford Foundation, were commuters to New York City from this privileged West-chester community. Hill had had a distinguished agricultural career at Cornell University before joining Ford, and the two men found themselves thinking along parallel lines.

Planning an international institute is an around-the-clock preoccupation and those who worked with Harrar and Hill were impressed that coming and going they could scarcely think of another subject. Harrar from the start had another ally, Dr. Warren W. Weaver, then Vice President for Natural and Agricultural Sciences at the Rockefeller Foundation. Weaver retired before the program was launched, but he and Harrar were responsible for much of the planning within the Rockefeller Foundation. Weaver brought to their discussions intellectual powers of the first order, and prestige and stature within and outside the Foundation. He and Harrar were a formidable pair within the one foundation as were Hill and Harrar in linking Ford and Rockefeller thinking. The three men surveyed prospects in Asia much as the "three Musketeers" had in Mexico. Enthusiasts all, they were tough-minded and rigorous, partly because this was their style and partly because they knew this venture was far more revolutionary than single-country programs. It was an experiment which broke with most copybook rules in foreign assistance. It originated in Scarsdale, not Los Baños; it involved little if any commitment from the Philippines, and it did not build, in the first instance, on indigenous strength. A colleague in the foundation world has observed: "If field representatives or New York staff had been polled, they would have been nearly unanimous in opposing it." However, the "conceptualizers" were ahead of the times and of their colleagues and they saw the moment in history had come for a single concentrated effort dedicated to improving the quality and production of rice, the basic food for more than half the world's people.

Once again, however, the main burden of leadership fell to one man, Dr. Robert F. Chandler, who in 1959 became the first director of IRRI. Formerly president of the University of New Hampshire, Chandler inspired confidence and generated interest wherever he went. Before settling down at Los Baños he had traveled extensively throughout Asia, recruiting an essentially all-Asian staff and both learning and sharing knowledge as he went. A prodigious worker and charismatic leader, Chandler put his stamp on IRRI as Harrar had on the Mexican project. They shared one characteristic that has sometimes gone unnoticed, given their great strengths in other areas. Both are men of insatiable intellectual curiosity; for them to live is to learn. When years later the staff of IRRI were asked, in connection with the appointment of a successor to Dr. Chandler, about his qualities, they observed to a man: "He made it his business to keep abreast of our research and we never knew when he would confront us with a probing question that went to the heart of our field."

If there were similarities in the men there also were differences between Mexico and IRRI. The cost of the Mexican program over the first decade of its history was less than $2 million—which, in Raymond Fosdick's words, represented "a trifling cost . . . weighed against the results accomplished." Compared with this, IRRI, which was able to move ahead rapidly, building on the knowledge and experience of the Mexican program, represented a substantial investment from the start. Thanks to the Ford Foundation, it was able to begin its work with a $7 million plant. Its annual budget of $1.5 million approached that of the total spent in the first decade of the Mexican program. The goal was to bring together in one place all that was known about rice and to experiment with new varieties that could double, triple, or quadruple rice production in various Asian countries. Each year the Institute became a more powerful tool for the alleviation of hunger, and its "miracle rice" has changed the picture of rice production in many countries of Asia. The variety that was first released was not without problems. It was coarse and brittle and not easily prepared to suit the palates of some Asians. But IRRI, after more than five years of experimentation, needed a success story if its varieties were to be applied and adapted throughout Asia. It found it in IR-8 and continued with other successor varieties, all tested with painstaking care against all the contingencies of pests and disease that could be anticipated.

The success story remains in midpassage, but certain conclusions appear self-evident. The Philippines, as Mexico and West Pakistan in wheat, has become self-sufficient in rice (the years 1970–72, with damaging storms and blight, were the exceptions). India seems to be approaching this goal. The Institute has launched an upland rice

77

production project under the leadership of the indestructible "musketeer," Dr. Richard Bradfield, as well as a project on rice production in deep-water areas. Its staff has fanned out to help in other countries and, as Harrar and Hill envisaged, its influence has spread throughout Asia.

A project that would have been impossible if leaders had played by the book has come to serve a continent and the whole world because they had the courage to change the rules. Moreover, when the program was launched, detractors argued that no other groups had committed themselves to aid the project. Supporters countered that the achievements of IRRI would draw other resources. This was to be a prophecy fulfilled, for—as they had dreamed might be true—project grants flowed in from U.S. AID, the Philippine National Science Development Board, the American Potash Institute, the Canadian International Development Agency, and herbicide and pesticide companies. U.S. AID joined the Ford and the Rockefeller Foundations in supporting the core program in 1969, and the World Bank and other financial institutions have signaled their future interest and support.

The single most important lesson emerging is that international agricultural efforts in the private sector have bought time. They have given hope that at least for the next generation famine and starvation may be staved off and hunger alleviated if not conquered. They have bought time in the race with population, perhaps twenty years. The programs have been of a piece, starting small, growing, and reaching out. And this after all is the essential purpose of demonstration projects or pilot programs in the private sector.

POSTSCRIPT TO THE GREEN REVOLUTION

The successes of the "green revolution" and the changing circumstances under which it is evolving have stimulated "a great debate" among its defenders and its critics. As has so often been true, both sides in the debate run the risk of absolutizing their arguments, often for quite understandable reasons. The defenders see in the criticism an organized movement to undermine the continuation of their efforts. They point to the fact that there remain a billion and a half hungry people in the less-developed countries, some without enough to eat and others the victims of malnutrition. While the new high-yielding varieties enable a farmer to produce three to four times as much grain, the conquest of hunger for the world's people remains an unfinished task. There are needs beyond the major food grains and the only hope for forestalling famine over the next three decades will be to match the dramatic advances that were made in wheat, corn, and rice in the 1960's. Beyond this, population growth rates continue at unprecedented levels and make imperative the spread of new agricultural technologies if food production is to keep pace.

These self-evident needs have not, however, had the effect of silencing the continuing debate. For those who seek clarity and the truth, it is often difficult to judge either the substance or the debaters. Try as we may, few if any of us can stand back to view the exchange objectively. Some of us have what amounts to an ingrained suspicion of intellectuals and social critics whose main function so often seems to be to question, plant doubt,

79

and discredit. They are characteristically long on questions and short on action.

There are others who point to a tendency on the part of the true believers to assert that catastrophe will be averted only through a single approach to mankind's problems. At an earlier historical stage, it was universal free trade, worldwide democracy, or an international parliament that was the answer. None brought the world the promised utopia. It could be that those who adopt a single-factor approach, either to the conquest of hunger or to population control, are infected with the same disease. Many of them appear eager to have us believe, for example, that successes in increasing food production or in reducing population growth will eliminate the prospect of international conflict. However, there is little historical or contemporary evidence for their belief. Conflict is if anything more likely among those who have reached a minimum level of well-being and gained thereby the assurance and self-confidence to advance their claims. Tragically, conflict, when it breaks out, can destroy overnight the gains that have been made on other fronts. The inescapable lesson of history, then, is that it will not do to imagine that man will ever escape the need for grappling with his recurrent and perennial problems: hunger and disease, poverty and equality, warfare and justice. More significantly, however stubbornly crusaders hold to their mission, hope lies not in a campaign against a single problem but in the untiring and unending struggle for a better world.

The resolution of "the great debate" on the green revolution depends therefore on widening the sphere of discussion and an integration of approaches to mankind's problems. If anyone doubts the urgency of controlling international conflict and its relevance to the conquest of hunger, he need only reflect on the Indo-Pakistan conflict. India in 1968 increased its per acre yield of wheat 62 percent, thanks in part to the new varieties. West Pakistan appeared on the road to becoming self-sufficient in basic food grains. The outbreak of the conflict and the stark survival needs of millions of refugees flowing across boundaries threatened to overturn the spectacular gains that had been made. In a few days of fighting, conflict wiped out the miracles that had been wrought over the decades.

The need for a more integrated approach is even greater in other countries and areas. The increase in food production in the less-developed countries, thanks to the green revolution, is nothing if not spectacular. Ceylon increased its rice crop by 34 percent from 1968 to 1970. The Philippines, which for most of the twentieth century has imported rice, has been able in several of the most recent years to meet its own needs, saving millions of dollars in foreign exchange. Turkey, by using Mexican seed, achieved yields in 1967–68 more than double those of local wheat varieties. And the story is equally dramatic in other countries.

The major criticisms of the green revolution fall broadly into economic, political, and social categories. In a *New York Times* dispatch dated November 20, 1971, a special committee of the United Nations Food and Agriculture Organization was reported as stating that "increased productivity alone has not improved the lot of rural workers but on the contrary frequently makes it worse."[1] The distinguished committee, headed by Carlos Lleras Restrepo, a former president of Colombia, noted that "in India the introduction of new high-yield varieties had greatly reduced the immense food deficits but social tensions had increased."[2] This view of the relationship between the distributional impact of the high-yielding varieties and the formation of new political alignments in India is most dramatically illustrated in a recent book by Dr. Francine Frankel.[3]

The potentially harmful economic effects of the green revolution have received by far the most attention in the great debate. Basically, the dissenters argue that the successful application of the high-yielding varieties requires considerable financial resources and/or easy access to credit in order to purchase the necessary complementary inputs, such as fertilizer, tube wells and the like. Given the already wide disparities in agricultural income distribution between the large and small landowners, it is argued that the necessity to have ready access to needed capital and financial resources threatens to bias the benefits of the green revolution to the already prosperous, large landowners. It can, therefore, exacerbate the rural income distribution problem of developing nations.

A second major component of the argument of the

[1] *New York Times,* November 21, 1971, p. 10.

[2] *Ibid.*

[3] Francine R. Frankel, *India's Green Revolution: Economic Gains and Political Costs* (Princeton, N.J.: Princeton University Press, 1971).

economic dissenters relates to the employment and unemployment implications of the green revolution. The argument basically takes the following form: It is asserted that the new varieties are subject to considerable economies of scale, especially when applied through mechanized production techniques, so that there is a built-in tendency for the larger farmers to gain a decided competitive advantage over their counterparts on smaller landholdings. This phenomenon can only lead, so it is claimed, to the eventual consolidation of land in the hands of a few, while the many are driven off their land to swell the ranks of the rural underemployed or, more likely, to join the armies of urban unemployed. Unlike the historical experience of Western Europe and the United States, however, the ability of the urban industrial sector of less-developed nations to absorb these "surplus" farm workers is extremely limited. Thus, it is claimed by some that the green revolution has within itself the seeds for a potential "red revolution" as the vast armies of the rural and urban unemployed begin to assert their claim to a fair share of the fruits of economic progress.

Clearly, it is as naive and myopic to lay the blame for widespread political and social unrest on a single factor such as the green revolution as it is for its proponents to make equally exaggerated claims about the economic bonanza that societies will reap from the harvest of the green revolution. The fact of the matter is that there is nothing inherent in the new technology of grain production per se which necessarily should lead to more unequal distributions of farm income or more widespread rural and urban unemployment. If income disparities widen greatly and unemployment rises sharply, it will be due more to defective governmental policies with regard to distribution and application of the new varieties and their complementary inputs than to the nature of the new varieties themselves. To take a simple example, empirical studies of the new rice varieties have shown (1) that they are equally adaptable to small and large farms and (2) that their net employment effects are neutral to slightly positive, with the increased demand for labor as a result of multiple cropping offsetting the decreased demand for labor in land preparation. The argument may be true that in areas where the new varieties have been most successfully adapted, such as the Indian Punjab, there has been a tendency for greater income disparity and less employment. However, these phenomena are probably due not so much to the new varieties themselves as to the policy framework in which they have been applied. Specifically, policies that encourage premature tractor mechanization through special tax concessions, overvalued exchange rates, and various questionable import arrangements, all of which artificially cheapen the price of imported capital equipment, probably contribute more to the undesirable income and employment effects than the technology of high-yielding food grains.[4]

---

[4] It is interesting to note in this regard that a recent paper by Dr. Randolph Barker and his associates at IRRI has shown that whereas tractor mechanization on large farms has lowered labor inputs, it has not lowered unit production costs. See Barker *et al.*, *Employment and Mechanization in Philippine Agriculture* (Geneva: ILO, October 1971).

Thus, as so often happens in "great debates," both sides seem to lose sight of the basic issue toward which both have much to contribute. In the case of the green revolution this basic issue is how the spectacular achievements of the new technology of food production can best be applied so as to achieve the *multiple* objectives of greater yields, higher incomes more widely distributed, and greater employment opportunities. These objectives are clearly attainable. They can be realized, however, only through a cooperative effort on the part of agricultural and social scientists working together in an environment in which both sides appreciate the significance of each other's contributions to the common effort.

# 5: THE DEBATE OVER ECONOMICS IN THE DEVELOPING COUNTRIES

A recurrent theme in "the great debate" over the transferability of lessons from success stories such as "the green revolution" is whether similar progress can be made in more sensitive social areas. The key questions center around whether priority problems can be defined, "solutions" pursued with singularity of purpose, and whether the parties view cooperative programs as likely to lead to mutually acceptable "solutions." Doubts are often expressed whether any social enterprise can have the sharp and continuing focus of, say, the Mexican Agricultural Program, or the International Rice Research Institute. Skeptics ask whether diverse social groups will accept the results of programs of social change that may upset or affect their class and position. For it is axiomatic with most socioeconomic endeavors that some gain and others lose. Oftentimes part of the solution requires that privileged groups give up what they may have. Thus, what is lacking with social projects is the universal appeal of increased food production or improved health.

On the other hand, is it not fair to ask how the gains and losses are spread across society, even in scientific, medical, and agricultural activities? For example, there has been much debate recently about the social and economic impact of the green revolution. In the initial instance, at least, the principal beneficiaries tend to be the large farmers who have sufficient land and capital to purchase the necessary complementary inputs of the hybrid varieties, such as fertilizer and irrigation facilities. The smaller farmers, whose access to credit is often limited, may be unable to compete. The potential therefore exists for these small farmers to be driven off their land or bought out by larger farmers. They will then be forced to migrate to the cities and swell the ranks of the urban unemployed unless attempts are made to provide attractive rural alternatives to farming. Therefore, when technological breakthroughs take place the crucial issue in the long-term, even for health or agriculture, is what social use will be made of the discovery, even though there may be spectacular short-run results from making this change.

Notwithstanding, certain social problems urgently need study and action, whatever their complexity. Three examples of social problems crying for such review illustrate what may be necessary and possible. One is the need for an intensive international effort to investigate the cultural, socioeconomic, and institutional bottlenecks standing in the way of acceptance of birth control in different developing nations. The knowledge which an inquiry such as this could produce might provide new insights into the mechanism through which the perceived interests of the population are translated into those behavioral patterns which constitute the major determinants of the use of new biological materials. A small beginning has been made in this area, but much more needs to be done. And unless it is done a large part of the population-control field will remain untouched, thereby limiting the applicability of all other research in the field.

Another area is indigenous entrepreneurship. In a country like Indonesia there are fewer than five hundred modern private entrepreneurs; even if the number were doubled, they would fall far short of contemporary national needs. However, at the provincial level thousands of smaller enterprises demonstrating competence and achievement have been in existence for many years. A crucial question is how are these latent forces to be given the necessary redirection so that they can contribute in a much greater way to the development process? What about the knowledge, psychology, and institutional bottlenecks in the overall environment or the financial institutions that limit or serve this group? Knowledge collected about indigenous entrepreneurs might be applied to assist development in a much broader sense than the simple growth in national output.

A third area is the growing worldwide problem of rural and urban unemployment and, even more importantly, underemployment. The vast underutilization of human resources is a problem which is identifiable and susceptible of interdisciplinary review. However, while no government is for massive unemployment, there may be many in society, ranging from trade unionists to wealthy capitalists, who could be affected adversely by a genuine governmental effort to stimulate significant new job creation. Because not everyone benefits, therefore, a governmental administration may table the problem. To stimulate governmental action, the threat of a major social dislocation may be necessary. The social incentives to use the "solutions" scientists produce are often limited by the political interests and economic positions of the citizenry. For these and other reasons, a society's attitude toward unemployment, entrepreneurship, and population may be different in kind from food or health.

Nevertheless, the arguments against the easy transferability of successful approaches to food and health having been made, a growing number of concerned leaders are persuaded that urgent social problems can no longer be ignored. In fact, it can be argued that unless the developing societies, in conjunction with public and private donor agencies, intensify their efforts to solve the population-unemployment dilemma, the fruits of past scientific and technological progress may be rapidly dissipated. On population, someone has quipped: "How many ladybugs can you put in a jar before they stop being ladies?"

If the economic kinetic energy which at present is bottled up in the educated but unemployed youth of any society is not released, that society will not gain a place in the international firmament. It is regrettable in the story of international cooperation that there are so few cases of an organization or state selecting a social problem for study and action—and staying with it over a period of ten or twenty years. Too often we speak of "doing the social sciences"—instead of focusing all the knowledge and skills of related social sciences toward resolving a problem. At the very least, the effective training and/or utilization of growing but idle human resources, which constitute an asset of great potential value, would seem a rational objective. Perhaps the single greatest impact of the Mexican Agricultural Program was the training of more than seven hundred Rockefeller Foundation scholars, one hundred fifty to one hundred seventy-five as Ph.D.'s. These are the men who are guiding Mexico today, who have the confidence of political and military leaders, and who build for the future. Our aim is to demonstrate in the examples that follow that a training enterprise such as this is possible in other fields—"freeing the latent and kinetic energy" present in developing countries.

Before turning to the case study that presents the most convincing evidence for the transfer of knowledge and skills in the social sciences, namely economics, we should make at least passing reference to the "great debate" which presently is raging within scholarly organizations in the United States. High on the agenda of recent annual meetings of virtually every professional organization in the social and humane sciences has been the controversy between the "scientists" and the "activists." Their differences create a serious intellectual cleavage that divides each major scholarly group. The former point to the advances that have been made, particularly in the behavioral sciences, in creating discrete and autonomous disciplines that provide the tools of analysis and research for rigorous and systematic inquiry. They deplore the criticism of the new disciplines. They call for more—not less—commitment to the canons of science: objectivity, precision, measurement, testing, and theory-building. The goal in the first instance is the advancement of knowledge through the testing of hypotheses, the refinement of methodologies, and the development of relevant conceptualization.

The activists, for their part, identify and exploit a widespread and far-reaching concern in our crisis-ridden society that science alone cannot save us. They point to the urgent social issues threatening society, to which behavioral scientists are largely indifferent. They mention race and Vietnam, population and environment, and poverty and youth. "Social scientists fiddle while the republic burns." The behaviorists, the critics charge, are beguiled by the rewards of technical sophistication; the result is the piling up of more and more knowledge on issues of less and less significance. The rallying cry around which the activists have organized their campaign is "relevance." What will it profit the world if the social scientists become scientists by withdrawing from the real world and its overriding problems?

The activists go one step further, however, and assume the role of social critics, if not social revolutionaries. Drawing on Marx, they proclaim that their task is not merely to describe but to change society. With or without studies and research, they assert, we already know that present-day society is corrupted. The behaviorists neglect the place of values in society, preening themselves on attaining value-free social science. The activists embrace values with a vengeance. They are supremely confident that their values are those which will transform society. They explain the shortcomings of the world in terms of its failure to accept their values. If behaviorists ignore values, activists oversimplify them. What behaviorists and activists have in common is the lack of the spirit of inquiry and reflection which characterized the world's great philosophies. The most telling comparisons arise from the differences between behaviorism or activism, on the one hand, and the Socratic dialogue on the other. The former assumes that there is no need for open-ended contemplation of values and that final answers are at hand to the perennial problems of justice and power, the people and authority, and the best form of government. For the latter, the form and purpose of the dialogue is questioning, inquiry, and conversation. Justice and authority are timeless problems and the search for the best form of government an unending pursuit of what is good in the context of a given time and place. There are no final answers, but there are higher principles against which current social realities can be measured and understood.

Thus the social science disciplines are in flux. Even if the above description of the two major schools of behavioral and activist social sciences is exaggerated and overdrawn (there are of course shadings and varying degrees of emphasis in each of the schools), the continuing debate goes on. The two schools unquestionably represent two extremes, but extremes that from the standpoint of numbers and justifications appear dominant. Surely they outnumber the more old-fashioned schools such as those of social philosophy or problem-solving. No one would question that they have contributed, but each would seem to be the victim of an extreme. The tendencies and excesses of behaviorism and activism cause anxiety that American and Western social sciences have less to offer the rest of the world than had been hoped. And for those who view the American professional and scholarly scene from other lands with other values and needs, the anxiety becomes even more acute.

The more positive consequences of a self-critical approach to the transfer of American social science skills to other cultures may be to keep in check an American attitude that has often hampered our relations with the rest of the world. Our messianism and moral self-righteousness has sometimes made us unsufferable to other peoples; we were "God's chosen people" placed on this earth to teach other men truth and virtue. Our moralism has, of course, never been a national monopoly. The Greeks, Romans, Spanish, French, and British before us, and the Russians and Chinese in our day have been similarly infected. Yet only among equals can there be full sharing; we need to be aware that we bring to any partnership both strengths and weaknesses, contributions and limitations. Our "sciences" may benefit others but may also profit in turn from the changing social context in which they must be tested and applied. When we come to see that we can both contribute and learn, we may give more than when we see ourselves as absolute and omniscient.

Economics, to be sure, has suffered less from the cleavage between behaviorists and activists than other social science disciplines, but it has not been immune.

## The Debate over Economics

The disappearance of political economy is one example of the passing focus of economics on the hard issues in the public and private economic order. Many of the troublesome problems that continue to haunt us are not merely economic or political or sociological. If this is true in highly organized and developed societies in which powerful forces come together in clearly differentiated sectors such as the economy, it is true *a fortiori* in less-developed ones where religion, politics, and economics merge.

Nevertheless, our friends abroad, seeking the fruits of modernization and economic development, request help in the creation of cadres of qualified economists. There is an urgent need for professional economists; some form of economic planning is pursued in each newly emerging nation-state. As high priority was given to the need for doctors and agriculturalists a decade ago, the demand for economists and engineers is emphasized today.

Economics of course is one sphere in which the training of leadership often has been successfully pursued. There are successful case studies in the Philippines, India, Israel, Indonesia, Thailand, Nigeria, and Chile. The rationale for concentrating initially on training economists among the social sciences is that these are the individuals who are likely to be most called upon by their governments to chart the course of national development for many years. They must be able to translate social objectives into viable economic programs under the constraint of limited national resources. It is therefore essential that they have a firm grounding in economic analysis and quantitative methods. Their task, however, is in many ways much more difficult than that of their counterparts in the agricultural sciences. They cannot operate in a unimodal framework in which, for example, increasing farm yields is the single overarching objective. Society is their laboratory and, by nature, the social fabric consists of many competing interests and objectives. Choices between industrial modernization or rural development, between increased mechanization or more labor-intensive enterprises, or between inflation or unemployment must constantly be evaluated.

It follows that training in economics per se cannot guarantee that the correct decisions will invariably be made. Unless the individual economist has a broad understanding and appreciation of the social, political, and cultural milieu in which his decisions must be made, he is apt to leave out many essential noneconomic variables from his decision framework. This is why visiting economists and technical advisors so often fail. It also underlines the urgent need to train indigenous scholars of broad vision with the "tools" of economics so that they may sensibly and sensitively select those tools which are particularly applicable to the needs of their societies and transfer this knowledge to future generations of university scholars, government advisors, and private entrepreneurs.

Americans have had a modicum of success in helping to train young economists and create viable departments of economics abroad. The search for young economists capable of benefiting from training abroad involves a painstaking assessment of their capacity for rigorous and exacting study, as well as their commitment to national development. Once they return to their "home university" they need, as with other "conceptualizers," some kind of mutual protection society. Otherwise, as was the case in Chile before the launching—with the support of the International Cooperation Administration—of a cooperative program between Catholic University in Santiago and the University of Chicago, they are vulnerable professionally and politically. A major weakness of Catholic University had been the lack of any full-time program with positions carrying status and salary, and the resultant draining of the university for attacks on a host of immediate problems in the private and public sectors. The University of Chicago, as a condition of its assistance to Catholic University, insisted on the establishment of seven or eight full-time professorships to which the men it would train might return. To the extent that the Department of Economics at Catholic University has weathered the present political crisis, it is because of the full professional status of an appointment at the University. To ignore this requirement is to invite political vulnerability and erosion of professional expertise.

Thus, for economics, the problem of objectivity remains a major but not an insoluble problem in the developing countries. There are so few economists that they are too often drawn into part-time government work. Once they become "operators" in this sense of the word, they are taking the risk that their personal careers and the reputations of their academic departments could suffer from being identified with unpopular or unsuccessful policies. While it would not be reasonable to suggest that all academic

97

economists remain uninvolved in government policy-making, it is clearly important that each nation preserve a core of highly skilled professional economists who have the independence to join with other intellectuals in analyzing the nation's problems and policies for the future.

A central issue in the training of economists outside of their home country is whether they are, in fact, enabled thereby to develop knowledge and techniques which can be applied to the problems of their own country. One trend of thought has emphasized that questions of public policy and development strategy are not in the framework of economics and that the results will be bad if the nation's leaders depend too much on economics. A society seeking an economic goal may, for reasons of policy, be unwilling to face the allocation questions essential in reaching that goal. It is unrealistic to expect that economics can do more than define what is necessary in allocating resources to achieve certain goals. Economists, according to this line of reasoning, should stick to their knitting and function as economists and not as decision-makers, although their analyses may be relevant to national problems.

An opposing viewpoint, which seems to be more widely held than its counterpart, says that economists must seek "indigenous" roots in their training and approach in order to produce knowledge that can be applied to national problems. They cannot escape responsibility for national policy. In their training, this may require that dissertations be written on their own soil, that courses in the history of science be pursued to lend perspective on how disciplines are changed and adapted over time, that new methods be evolved for speeding the transfer of knowledge, and that indigenous institutions resist sending local students for training below the Ph.D. level to Western universities. The graduate program in economics at the University of the Philippines or at the Catholic University of Chile, for example, may be a better alternative for early training for students from Asian or Latin American countries than immediate graduate work in the United States.

The counter-argument is that building a program on this basis would lead to a development institute but not to economics. What is needed instead is the strongest, most rigorous training of young scholars in economic theory and in specialties in economics such as international trade. There is a core to economic theory essential and similar for every country. Local changes in the way theory is taught or applied are not changes in theory itself, and the first task in preparing economists is to prepare them in economic theory, requiring work at strong international centers. An amendment to this view is to note that certain areas of theory have been neglected in the United States, (for example, the theory concerning infrastructure institutions and the functioning of the economy on an interim basis without them). Moreover, much of the existing theory as taught in American universities is predicated upon a set of institutional and behavioral assumptions which may not be valid for developing societies. For example, the Keynesian theory of unemployment and the policy prescriptions for alleviating this dilemma are in many instances irrelevant for the situation in Africa, Asia, and Latin America. American economists engaged in the training of "third-country" economists also may overlook dimensions that have priority within the developing state.

At least part of the debate between the two approaches may be academic. It now seems unlikely that American and European universities can train the number of economists required in the developing countries. Therefore, whatever the blend of economics and development studies that mark programs outside of these areas, the indigenous institutions will, to an increasing degree, have to play a more important role in training their own economists.

A provincial, as distinct from a national, university in a developing country often can contribute most by concentrating on the development of its own region. For example, the government of Indonesia has depended upon newly created faculties of economics in outlying universities, such as Hasanuddin University in Makassar, for preparing the development plan for their regions. In Colombia, the faculty of economics at the Universidad del Valle has performed a similar function for the Cauca Valley. Within a region, the need is at least as urgent as it is nationally for economists to be sheltered and detached from politics, both to preserve objectivity and professionalism, and to make them less vulnerable to external demands and pressures. If economists are to emerge as leaders, the rules concerning the dynamics of the two kinds of leadership cannot be overlooked.

However, the dilemma of using as over against protecting economists is very real, and the need to use them may in fact be desperate in some countries. Despite the fact that they do not have broad competence in the field of social and political policy, economists have been sources for urgently needed study and advice. If they lose something as pure economists by taking policy positions, they gain as political economists. The issue, of course, which authorities like Professor Theodore Schultz would raise, is whether a Ph.D. in economics is the best training for someone occupying a policy position in a developing country. Even if it should be, the question would remain whether the optimum use of a fully trained economist is as a full-time "operator."

Indeed the question is sometimes raised whether a professional economist, in view of his training and skills, is more like a mathematician or physicist than a doctor or lawyer. Is economics more concerned with the mastery of theory than of human beings and institutions? There is an important and influential body of economists who would say that economics is akin to chemistry and physics in its theoretical power. Yet somehow developing societies in their needs all expect more from economists than mere knowledge of their discipline, although this expectation is crucial in itself.

Thus, the problem of the adequacy of training economists to be leaders of the national development process remains one for inquiry, discussion, and study. An answer to the question of the social implications of economic projects in developing countries may depend on one's definition of economics. The sensitivity about economics as a proper subject for external assistance diminishes to the extent economics is more scientific and theoretical and less social and applied, but the problem of poverty and of pressing human need may make it unrealistic to seek so detached and transcendent a status for the economist. In the resolution of this issue, the debate about cooperative programs in volatile social areas will have to be resolved and worked out. Economists trained in the United States and Europe are today on the firing line in planning agencies in Indonesia and India. Their decisions will have profound implications for these countries. Yet if they are to continue to function through successive stages in the evolution of their nations' policies, they ought to be viewed whenever possible as "conceptualizers," whose usefulness depends on their serving their nation as economists, not as operators or policy-makers.

The dramatic successes that have greeted the efforts of foundation programming in agriculture are less immediately visible in economics, at least in part because of the nature of the two disciplines. However, the economic miracle that is Indonesia in the post-Sukarno era is inseparably linked with a brilliantly conceived and executed Indonesian–University of California project, financed by the Ford Foundation. It is a commentary on the possibilities of international cooperation that at a time of political and economic adversity and throughout the self-imposed isolation of President Sukarno's regime, when Indonesia withdrew from the United Nations and most national and international assistance activities in Indonesia were suspended, some fifty young Indonesians continued to pursue advanced studies in economics at California and Harvard Universities. Following the abortive revolution and the rise to power of General Suharto, many of these men were installed in positions of great responsibility in the government of Indonesia. The largest group was assigned to the Planning Agency (BAPPENAS), including the versatile and imaginative Dr. Widjojo as its head. Others went to the Ministries of Finance, Education, Agriculture, and International Trade. It would be difficult to find a comparable group anywhere in the world who in such a relatively brief time were so fully trained and prepared, and so intelligently employed for the skills they possessed. The result of their labors was a program of economic stabilization that has reduced annual inflation from a shattering 600 percent to less than 10 percent, through the use of well-known but little-used principles of economics. Similar progress has been made in improving Indonesia's position in international trade. If this Ford Foundation project was something less than a "green revolution," it was a revolution nonetheless, peacefully transforming the economic position of a key country in Asia. It is well to remember that the impetus came from a privately supported exchange and training program that proceeded according to plan at a time when almost every other public and international program had ground to a halt.

The plan itself deserves mention not least because the Indonesians themselves played so vital a role. Their blueprint for building up a critical mass of national economists was closely followed. Each year a specified number of carefully selected young Indonesians went abroad, knowing months in advance that they had been chosen. On completion of their training they returned to opportunities and positions for which similar planning had been done. The guiding spirit at home was the senior Indonesian economist, Dr. Sumitro, whom younger Indonesians describe as "the father of Indonesian economics." But one by one the younger men, such as the present Minister of Finance, Dr. Ali Wardana, joined Sumitro and made up a critical mass of able, well-trained professionals, respecting one another, working together, and forming, as it were, their own mutual protection society. For the 1970's it is impossible to exaggerate their importance to the nation's economy.

In the Philippines, a comparable development took place having even greater educational significance, if less direct and immediate effect on economic policy. Beginning in the early 1950's the Rockefeller Foundation undertook to join with the faculty of economics at the University of the Philippines in developing a first-class core group capable of training economists from the Philippines and other Asian countries, ultimately through the Ph.D. program. By the late 1950's, a small but highly competent staff had been trained and a regionally relevant M.A. program established, financed in large part by the Rockefeller Foundation. Malaysians, Koreans, Thais, Indonesians, and others sought places as degree candidates as neighboring countries discovered the value and economic advantage of training at a nearby regional center.

## The Debate over Economics

By the mid-1960's the University of Wisconsin, under the auspices of the Ford Foundation, assisted the University of the Philippines faculty to make the quantum leap from an M.A. to the Ph.D. level by committing themselves to provide three or four visiting professors each year, thus assuring training at a level that temporarily lay beyond the manpower resources of the local group. The guiding genius throughout this enterprise was the late Everett Hawkins, whose tireless contributions in the Philippines and Indonesia will be remembered for years to come. Rockefeller Foundation staff members and visiting professors from Western universities with Rockefeller financing worked easily with the Wisconsin staff, and today the completion of this major program is in sight. The foundations and those who have served under their banner predict that in a very few years their task will be completed and the Philippines capable of functioning on their own.

The success story of economics in the Philippines is a variation on a common theme. University of the Philippines faculty members, despite their numbers, have contributed substantially to public policy as advisors to government agencies, directors of development banks, members of the Council of Economic Advisors, and cabinet members. But with one or two exceptions, their public service has been temporary and short-term and they have invariably returned to their faculty base. More so than in Indonesia, they have been largely "conceptualizers," leaving to others the continuing task of "operating" and managing the public and industrial sectors. At

105

the same time, they, as their Indian counterparts at the Delhi School of Economics, have been in demand as visiting professors at American, British, and European institutions, emphasizing in this way the international character of their discipline and continually renewing and updating their knowledge.

One other success story that merits at least passing reference is that of the university in East Africa. In the early 1960's the Rockefeller Foundation joined the Inter-University Council in England to assist the three colleges in Uganda, Kenya, and Tanzania to build complementary centers of strength in economics. In Dar-es-Salaam, a fruitful working relationship was established from the beginning between the fledgling economics faculty, the Economic Research Bureau, and the economic planning arm of the government. Successive Rockefeller-sponsored visitors have served as heads of the faculty, the Economic Research Bureau, and the Bureau of Resource Assessment and Land Use Planning at the University. Experienced Western economists who have reviewed the cooperative effort in Tanzania express the view that in few African countries has economics been more operationally relevant. Similarly, in Kenya, Dr. James S. Coleman, Associate Director for Social Sciences of the Rockefeller Foundation, has served as Director of the Institute of Development Studies, a multi-disciplinary center engaged in policy-oriented studies of both scientific and practical use to the government. Indeed the link between IDS and the relevant government agencies and departments is such that public funding has been forthcoming for serious private studies on topics such as the electoral process, rural-urban migration, and priorities for accelerated rural development. The test of relevance at Makerere, the University College in Uganda, is best illustrated by noting that British, Russian, and other European advisors, as well as young Ugandan economists, regularly attended research seminars conducted by American and British economists on Rockefeller Foundation staff assignments. Rockefeller staff have worked out input-output tables for Uganda, contributed to work on the economic plan, and written textbooks and study materials for the study of economics in an African context.

Throughout these efforts and in good times and bad in overall East African relations with the West, the training of young Africans has gone on within the East African community. Every encouragement has been given to the development of a regional outlook, and movement of nationals from one country to another has been facilitated. Social science councils, located in each country and with travel funds from foundations, cooperated freely across national boundaries, establishing lasting functional relationships for the whole of East and Central Africa. Cooperation has been the hallmark of everything that outside bodies have encouraged, facilitated, and sponsored.

The story of private initiative and foundation assistance in economics is certainly another chapter in the annals of private philanthropy. In the longer run, the process which this private initiative set in motion may turn out to have an impact which, albeit less easily quantified, is equally important and lasting as similar efforts in the fields of health and agriculture.

# 6: INSTITUTION-BUILDING AND UNIVERSITY DEVELOPMENT

The most dramatic examples of international coopera-tion, as we have seen, involve mankind struggling to find answers to the most immediate and urgent problems, such as health and hunger. Yet urgent problems have a way of succeeding one another as the most intense and critical issues with which society must cope. Overpopulation takes the place of high infant mortality, and unemploy-ment that of food shortages. What is common to the challenge of each successive problem is the search for an institutional framework within which "solutions" can be found. For every problem the categories of need are essentially the same: trained and qualified leadership, relevant and testable methods and approaches, adequate and continuing material resources, and trust in those who labor toward "solutions." The fundamental need, of course, is for relevant institutional and educational struc-tures and programs.

Education has emerged as a first priority of the devel-oping countries and in cooperating the private sector has proceeded from a position of strength. For one thing, education has historically been a primary concern for the private foundations, as even their critics acknowledge. For another, the processes of educational development are slow-paced and long-term, and private bodies are more likely to have the freedom and flexibility to commit men and resources for significant periods.

At the heart of the movement in developing countries for educational assistance is the worldwide revolution of rising expectations. Peoples long resigned to chronic poverty, endemic disease, and ignorance are affirming their right to a larger share of the world's knowledge and abundance. Few would deny that cooperative educational programs have a long and, for the most part, respected history. Religious and humanitarian organizations can point to decades, even centuries, of participation in aid to less fortunate peoples, particularly in the fields of education and health. While it is difficult to disentangle evangelical and educational purposes, the latter have come to play an increasingly important role. Similarly, relief and emergency measures are becoming less dominant. Proceeding on the assumption that human history is more and more a race between education and catastrophe, secular and religious agencies are placing greater stress on the training of leaders, the spreading of literacy and modern techniques in agriculture, business, and other areas.

The stage for these joint efforts has also changed, with a shift from Europe to other parts of the world. In the immediate post–World War II years, Europe received about 90 percent of all help sent abroad by voluntary organizations, but by 1958 this proportion had dropped to less than half. Instead, Europe, the United States, and a few others have become partners in a worldwide mission to assist the less-developed countries.

Through the early 1960's, the movement of all foreign assistance from the rich to the poor countries did not exceed $5 billion a year, not including direct Russian aid to countries such as Egypt. It remained at an aggregate level equivalent to 2 to 3 percent of the total output of the underdeveloped countries and about 15 percent of their total export earnings. Foreign aid was variously estimated as constituting 30 percent of all capital formation for the underdeveloped countries, exclusive of China. The assistance contributed by the United States was less than one-half of one percent of its gross national product. For some European countries, such as France, the amount was proportionately higher, but for others, lower.

Those who called for substantial increases in the efforts of rich nations to aid the poor spoke of assistance approaching $10–20 billion per year. Such expansion, it was clear, required unity of effort and the formation of a consortium of donor states. The first prerequisite for providing resources on the scale required was a concerted and organized effort by the richer countries. The second was the creation of a social and economic infrastructure adequate to support rapid growth within the developing country. Lacking this, the underdeveloped country would be unable to utilize increased foreign aid. Trained leadership and qualified personnel thus become indispensable factors for economic growth.

Development specialists, who sometimes view educational development as a low pay-out investment as compared with the building of factories, have had to reevaluate priorities. In developing countries the need to build up human resources necessitates careful attention to the economics of education, as the OECD Development Center, which trains officials of developing countries, recognizes.

## CHANGING PATTERNS OF
## INTERNATIONAL EDUCATION

The United States, from its earliest history, has provided centers of education for the world's peoples. The flow of students to our shores began in 1784 with Francisco Miranda at Yale, a Venezuelan who was later to become a leader in his country's struggle for independence. The first Chinese student was Dr. Yung Wing, who also studied at Yale and returned to China in 1859. The founder of Doshisha University in Japan, Joseph Hardy Neesima, graduated from Amherst College in 1874. By 1904, a total of 2,673 students from abroad had enrolled in American colleges and universities. Aside from Canada, which led all the rest, the largest flow of students came from Mexico, Cuba, Japan, China, the Philippines, and from other Latin American countries. By 1920–21, the figures had risen to 6,901 students, principally from China, Canada, South America, Japan, the West Indies, Russia, Mexico, India, Africa, France, and Great Britain. Following World War II, the total increased to 10,341 students from ninety-nine countries, including a growing number from Western Europe, thus reversing the flow which in the nineteenth century had found American graduates continuing their intellectual journey in European centers of learning. By 1965–66, it approached 90,000 and by 1970–71 reached 144,708.

The benefits of an international exchange program coming to a focus in strong American institutions of higher learning have become obvious. A more than thirtyfold increase in half a century attests to the far-flung educational opportunities afforded in the United States. Yet serious observers call attention to certain accompanying problems. As in other aspects of American foreign relations, noble intentions are not always matched by careful and dispassionate planning. Airlifts of masses of undergraduate students from underdeveloped countries have lacked the careful preparation that marks better-organized international exchanges. The crucial questions surrounding the student's present and future needs often go unasked. Where can he obtain the best undergraduate training most relevant to future responsibilities in his country? Do his future employers in government, educational institutions, or business enterprises concur in his study plan? How will his educational experience be evaluated when he returns and to what extent has he received commitment of a future position? Few men possess a crystal ball that projects clear career lines in advance, but this can never excuse lack of forethought. The major casualties of this type of international exchange are the young people, cut adrift from their own culture and institutions primarily because neither they nor their sponsors gave thought to preparing moorings to which they might return. It must also be said that certain zealous, though well-intentioned, spokesmen for cultural exchange are also at fault. Through encouraging young people to give heed only to attractive present educational prospects, they discourage a judicious weighing of future implications.

Beyond this, international exchange is undergoing a basic and far-reaching reappraisal in major Western countries. The fact is that the thoroughgoing studies and fundamental inquiries on which to base conclusions are lacking. There is need for a "Conant study" on international student exchange. We have impressions but little hard data on the effects of mass student exchange programs—for example, of Chinese students in the 1920's and 1930's. (Given the recent events in Sino-American relations, such a study may soon be possible.) For the present, therefore, impressions must take the place of solidly grounded conclusions. Acknowledging that present judgments are more intuitive than systematic, the quality and significance of large-scale and sometimes indiscriminate exchanges remain in doubt. The image is widespread of the rootless, denationalized, and detribalized student, alienated from the folkways and customs of his people, made accustomed to social and scientific affluence, disoriented by preoccupation with techniques and concerns of little relevance to his own society, and progressively drawn apart from genuine service to his community and nation.

Partly in reaction to this situation, a new pattern of

international education is emerging. Its stage is the home country of the foreign student, not the United States. The actors, as in the past, are masses of students and their professors and young instructors—joined in a common endeavor. Their purpose is better education, more closely linked to the needs of a particular people. The movement is reversed, for whereas in the earliest phase of international exchange, foreign students journeyed to the United States, now American professors are taking up residence at foreign institutions around the world. Their task remains that of educating foreign students—now, however, not in an American, but in their own cultural setting. As partners, not observers, Americans have joined national and expatriate educators in institution-building within another social and political context. They become part of the fabric of a society which has the power to use or misuse, assimilate or isolate, welcome or reject the graduates of the newly emerging educational process. They live and labor on the front line of an educational system which is evolving to meet local needs and prepare leaders for national responsibilities. They exchange the role of American critics standing in judgment on other educational systems for that of participants in social and educational invention, seeking to blend and adapt separate but compatible traditions of learning. If the education they provide is irrelevant to society's needs, they share the responsibility for failure. A key question is: When has an outside agency done its job and when should it turn to other areas?

The consequences that flow from the new pattern of

international exchange call for reflection, analysis, and review. First, the primary target of intellectual cooperation has shifted. It has become, in the first instance, institution-building. The lesson of a century of experience in the business of international exchange is that educating individuals is not enough. Every private and public agency has its warehouse of files recounting the melancholy experiences of individuals whose intellectual formation abroad left little to be desired but who, on returning, found scant outlet for their talents. Where the appropriate educational and scientific framework was missing, writers became clerks, economists became bank tellers, and scientists became salesmen. Coffee houses in the Middle East and Africa abound with economically displaced lawyers, accountants, and teachers. A much-quoted slogan for talent-hunters has been: "Find the bright and promising individual for study abroad and the future will take care of itself." Like many slogans, this guideline is too simple and tells less than half the story.

Responsibility for the selection of individuals for study in the United States is not easily or rapidly discharged. Such a choice is always a serious and awesome task. Some ivory-hunters are more successful than others in identifying excellence, as the records of men like Henry Allen Moe of the Guggenheim Foundation and the late Walter Rogers of the Institute of Current World Affairs make plain. Leaders of the Rockefeller Foundation periodically remind officers that since only a few are chosen, recipients of Foundation fellowships should be judged both as scholars and as prospective leaders in their fields.

116

Moreover, responsibility is not discharged through the identification of excellence alone. Especially in the developing countries, the question must be asked: What are the chances of a man trained in this specific field pursuing his subject? Some countries need general practitioners and paramedical personnel, but only a few are ready for specialists in open-heart surgery. Is it responsible for grant-making agencies to submerge the scholarly community of a country in educational opportunities unrelated to its most pressing needs? On the other hand, should it deny a man training for which he is eminently qualified simply because—in the agency's view—his country cannot yet use him as efficiently as might be wished?

When people identify persistent needs which must be met through efforts either by the private or public sector, institutions spring up to provide organized ways of coping with problems. Modernization in democratic and nondemocratic systems alike has brought with it large-scale social aggregation. Mass societies tend to create administrative units in which separate and arbitrary choices are subordinated to routine procedures and tables of organizations. Education is no exception to this trend toward bureaucratization. Hopefully, societies retain flexibility in the operation of large-scale organizations, but the outside agency which would assist must, for the most part, work within them. Moreover, trained personnel must find their place in the social organization of a particular country, and those who would foster further training are obliged to know as much about institutions as about individuals. It is as irresponsible to appraise

117

individuals and not the institutions in which they must work as to consider institutions and disregard the quality of individuals.

The most successful fellowship programs of private foundations have been those in which the individuals have, at the termination of a period of study abroad, had an assured institutional home. Particularly noteworthy are the fellowships awarded by the Rockefeller Foundation for agriculture in Mexico, social sciences in Europe, and medical and natural sciences in Europe and Latin America. Seven hundred young Mexicans, trained in leading American and Mexican schools of agriculture, have returned to responsible positions in the Ministry of Agriculture or in institutions such as the Graduate School at Chapingo. European social scientists who studied in American graduate centers while on leave from national institutions of higher learning today occupy a high proportion of social science professorships on the Continent. The experience of medical and natural scientists from Europe and Latin America chosen for Rockefeller Foundation fellowships is another case in point. In 1960, Foundation officers, reviewing a representative sample of a thousand fellows, discovered that all but one had returned to their native countries—a tribute to the careful screening, strict requirement of an institutional affiliation at the time of interview, and repeated discussions by Foundation officers with institutional leadership. This record, drawn from the history of one foundation, reflects a common experience of those who administer fellowships. The evidence is clear that there is no substitute for rigorous and systematic procedures giving equal attention to both sides of the equation, namely, the individual and his institution.

A second consequence resulting from the changing patterns of international exchange is the shift to an emphasis on graduate education for foreign students. Nothing could be more self-defeating than an approach to intellectual cooperation that couples institution-building in developing countries with large-scale exchanges that drain local institutions of the flower of the student population. Yet to a considerable extent, American agencies often find themselves working at cross-purposes in countries with fledgling institutions of higher education. For example, officials of universities in East Africa have periodically complained that places in their colleges were going unfilled at a time when undergraduate fellowships for study in the United States were multiplying. The facts are in dispute, and the truth hard to come by; it is argued that many young Africans admitted for study in American institutions cannot gain admission to African universities because of the stringency of educational requirements. To deny them the opportunity to study in American institutions is to deny them a college education. This flow may have been sharply curtailed in recent years, but the fundamental problem remains with us whenever we undertake to assist in institutional development. It would appear that a state of equilibrium gradually emerges as indigenous institutions are strengthened.

Few dispute the fact, however, that, generally speaking, a solid undergraduate degree from a recognized institution in the student's native country carries advantages. It enables him to study with those who must furnish his country's leadership. Ties of mutual respect and national self-consciousness form around a common educational experience. A greater awareness of the nation's problems and its human resources develops in its own classrooms and on its playing fields. The curriculum is more likely to be relevant, and education more likely to extend into local communities to meet pressing social needs. Finally, an institution with sufficient prestige to train its native sons is on the way to earning the right to serve the economy and the state.

If institution-building in developing countries leads to a certain de-emphasis on undergraduate training abroad, the opposite is true of graduate study. Few, if any, new universities are prepared for full-fledged graduate programs. Professional schools, more likely than not, lack resources. With the explosion of knowledge and the growing complexity of advanced subject matter in major fields, it is asking too much of infant universities that they simultaneously mount undergraduate and graduate programs. Even older universities in developing countries, such as the University of the Philippines, will probably limit themselves in most fields to M.A.-level courses, at least in the foreseeable future. Faculty development must precede the launching of across-the-board graduate training, though the pressures for building a complete university will doubtless increase.

Therefore, opportunities for graduate study in the United States for educational leaders from developing countries should be maintained and increased. For some, admission to the best graduate centers is immediately appropriate and attainable. Others may find their place in hand-tailored M.A. curricula at centers such as the Institute for Economic Development at Williams College or the University of Colorado Economics Institute. Others may require an intermediate year of intensive study in an outstanding liberal arts college. Latin American students slated for medical school have often profited greatly from a year of advanced undergraduate study in the basic sciences offered by Tulane University. The common theme underlying the study plans of foreign students across this broad spectrum is the quest for advanced learning or higher degrees. It seems likely that the United States will be called upon to assist more, not fewer, students in the realm of graduate and professional study.

A third consequence of the new form of international exchange relates to the role of visiting American faculty and of new forms of administrative assistance to the developing university. If the flow of masses of undergraduates to American universities is to be replaced by the movement of outstanding American educators to the new universities, considerable inventiveness and experimentation are called for. Most American scholars are not accustomed to a period of service abroad. Until fairly recently, expatriate scholars were predominantly British scientists and professors. Ironically, the demand for Americans appears concurrently with rising pressures and growing demands on the American scene. Britain, with its long tradition of international service, is caught up in

121

staffing the new universities in England. It remains true that Britain has gone further in building up cadres of career servants willing and able to operate on foreign soil. For example, the British Council has a permanent team of 120 English-language teachers available for overseas missions, whereas the United States must depend on term or contract personnel. The demise of the private agency, Education and World Affairs, which was created as a bridge between university and governmental leaders and an agency for recruitment is a sign of the limitations of the U.S. effort in this sphere.

As public programs, particularly those financed by the Agency for International Development (AID), have multiplied, the help of American universities has been enlisted. AID has undertaken to forge a partnership in technical assistance between itself, universities, and developing institutions. A report observes: "As of December 31, 1963, 72 universities in the United States were performing technical assistance tasks under 129 separate contracts with AID. More than $158 million was involved in those contracts."[1] As of June 30, 1970, AID is involved in the support of sixty-six universities through 119 contracts, with expenditures totaling $189 million. Collaboration by American universities in public programs is nothing new under the sun, for present relationships overseas are merely an extension of earlier

[1] John W. Gardner, *AID and the Universities: A Report to the Administrator of the Agency for International Development* (New York: Education and World Affairs, 1964), p. 1.

collaboration in such fields as national defense and agriculture. Universities have much to gain, for science and scholarship know no national boundaries and tomorrow's students must obtain a grasp of other cultures if they are to guide their nations in international relationships.

However, the common interests of AID and the universities in the outside world have not prevented frictions and misunderstandings, reviewed in detail in the celebrated Gardner Report.[2] This results partly from the long-term nature of the task. To paraphrase Woodrow Wilson, education, like politics, is the "slow boring of hard wood." Short-term contracts are not always productive of long-term results. In institution-building, three years should be viewed as a beginning and not the end of assistance. Someone has said that American foreign aid too often has involved responding to a twenty-year need with a three-year program, two-year personnel, and one-year appropriations. Universities are reluctant to undertake serious commitments when the means are not in sight of seeing the task to completion. In John Gardner's words:

> The universities say that AID lags far behind other agencies, such as the National Science Foundation. . . . AID responds that the universities make no attempt to understand its problems . . . universities have often acted irresponsibly—sending third-rate personnel overseas, neglecting the needs of the host country while they concentrate on what *they* want to do, . . . failing

[2] *Ibid.*

to put the full weight and resources of the university behind a contract and so on.[3]

From universities, a common complaint often repeated is that AID does little to strengthen their capabilities to work abroad. AID officials respond that, in the competition for scarce dollars, greater urgency attaches to aiding developing countries directly. University critics of AID policies reply that viewing assistance to American institutions as competitive with aid to foreign centers is short-sighted, for

> If the medical profession had insisted that every dollar spent in strengthening modern medical education, technology and science was a dollar unjustly diverted from the care of patients, we would still be treating fevers with leeches.[4]

This comparison may beg the question, however, for the real issue is how and where assistance to universities should be channeled. Is it general support that universities require, or aid to area-studies programs, or assistance to certain basic disciplines in the arts and sciences? It may be significant that, for some universities in their efforts overseas, strong departments in the basic sciences and social sciences play a more creative role in institution-building than area-studies centers, which may be exclusively research-oriented. It remains true that other governmental agencies, notably the National Science Foundation and the National Institutes of Health, have

[3] *Ibid.,* pp. 4–5.
[4] *Ibid.,* p. 12.

found ways of helping campus-based activities as related to overseas programs. It is unfortunately true, however, that assistance even through these respected channels has been sharply curtailed in recent years.

From the standpoint of effective assistance, the selection process in identifying American universities capable of contributing abroad is basic to all that follows. Authorities point to certain problems that hinder wise choices. On the one hand, certain universities may be overly aggressive in piling contract upon contract, beyond their ability to perform. On the other, those who make selections may be unfamiliar with universities in general or with strengths and weaknesses in particular fields. University men should appraise university potential. The quality of institutions and individuals who joined overseas in work of the International Health Division and the agricultural operating programs of the Rockefeller Foundation was a product of a simple selection formula. Basically, professionals were given the task of evaluating professionals. No scheme for a national clearinghouse nor for far-flung consortium operations nor the multiplying of detailed criteria can remove the importance of this simple rule. The test must be the professional competence of those who choose and firsthand knowledge of emergent needs in the developing institutions.

Controversy and disagreement have been greatest in the area of so-called university contracts. The extraordinarily attractive and seemingly logical principle of associating one American university with one developing university, through a so-called sister-university contract, has provoked widespread criticism, debate, and conflict. In John Gardner's words:

> Universities accuse AID of undue rigidity, incomprehensible delays, unsympathetic attitudes, and excessive and costly emphasis on small details. AID points out that universities have at times behaved irresponsibly and with little recognition of the requirements of accountability under which a government agency must function.[5]

Undoubtedly, much can be done to ease the possibility of conflict. The parties to the contract should strive for a complete understanding of the purposes of the joint enterprise and the responsibilities each assumes in the contract. Preliminary discussions can resolve points of difference, and visits by university people to the field clear away many false impressions. University leaders from the two centers should take part in the negotiations, and leaders with authority to make commitments must be signatories to the contract. Working scholars should be present at the takeoff if a crash landing is to be avoided. The anatomy of successful university contracts deserves study and analysis, and, as a starter, AID officials could do worse than to review the elements that have contributed to the effective working relationships and substantial success of partnerships such as the one between the University of Chicago and the Catholic University of Chile in economics. Clearly the pivotal role of Professor Theodore Schultz in both negotiation and leadership was

[5] *Ibid.*, p. 24.

126

a decisive factor. So perhaps was the focus on an identifiable and manageable discipline and the participation of first-class scholars. The teamwork between AID and the two universities was also crucial.

### LESSONS FROM PRIVATE
### EDUCATIONAL PROGRAMS ABROAD

By contrast with far-ranging public activities, experience confirms the wisdom of a private foundation's limiting its assistance to a relatively few universities in the developing countries. The extent of its resources and the nature of its experience justify this approach. Through concentrating foundation efforts, the possibilities of working together with the institution's top leadership in a spirit of mutual confidence are enhanced. Visiting scholars, whose service to overseas universities is made possible by the foundation, can tap the accumulated knowledge of their predecessors and of foundation officers. They can be sure that any contribution which they make will be central, rather than peripheral, to the development of their respective fields of knowledge. It is as professors, not as advisors, that they are called to serve. They are seen not as "intellectual adventurers" intruding on local academic programs, but as participants invited to join in carrying forward established studies or developing future curricula. One lesson that comes through from every university center at which help has been given is the importance of the visitor's natural functioning as a member of the particular scholarly com-

127

munity. He must become an accepted and integral part of the faculty, working within and not outside it. Because he is practicing the profession for which his credentials and experience best qualify him, he runs less risk of being seen as an alien force in a major national enterprise—education.

As the university development program moves ahead, requests for assistance in other spheres multiply. Since the goal has always been the strengthening of institutions as a whole, the need for reinforcing basic structures becomes self-evident. The fiscal and administrative infrastructure, although less visible, is as basic as the academic superstructure. Yet here it is easier to identify needs than to provide answers. A professor in physics or economics functions in broadly similar terms in any university. There are, of course, needs for new teaching materials and a syllabus organically linked with cultural patterns and the whole structure of evolving social and educational institutions. The best theoretical and descriptive writings must be adapted to changing local circumstances. At the center of the basic disciplines, however, whether in the physical or social sciences, is a hard core of concepts and principles to be taught and adapted. This seems less true of fiscal and administrative practices, especially when they are the outgrowth of different national or colonial traditions. The work of a registrar or estates officer in an African university is not the same as the task of a business manager elsewhere. The flow of items requiring action to the vice chancellor's desk may not be equal or similar in kind to those reaching a university president—

fortunately for the vice chancellor, our beleaguered university presidents would say. Efficiency and fiscal studies are useful, but many overseas institutions continue to look for more relevant types of surveys and better guidance on their implementation.

A few general principles, then, are illustrative of the lessons that derive from experience in the private sector. First, concentration is essential to assure the form and quality of assistance required. Obviously, foundations, in particular, lack the resources to scatter their assistance everywhere, but it becomes increasingly clear that governmental aid is also limited. In order for a recipient to benefit significantly, a certain critical mass of help is required, whether it takes the form of personnel, material resources, or capital. The leadership of developing institutions is quick to measure the extent of commitment of cooperating bodies. Comparisons are made between visitors who come to stay and those who never unpack their bags. Full and frank exchange of ideas is the result, not the forerunner, of mutual commitment. Yet intimate, unguarded, and self-critical discussion is vital if assistance is to make a difference. To mold a partnership in institution-building is to build a framework within which consultation goes on and mutually acceptable, far-reaching decisions are made. By contrast, casual involvement in institutional development results in hit-or-miss direction of those actions that shape the future. Whether the subject is selection of a fellow or reworking the syllabus or planning a new curriculum, the partners are engaged in what is ultimately the institution's most serious busi-

129

ness. Whether they succeed or fail depends on whether these topics are considered casually en route to the airport or through the solemn and deliberate processes of ongoing institutional life.

A corollary of the concentration principle stems from the weight of responsibility it throws on local leadership and national sponsors. In the same way that not every nation has made the hard decisions prerequisite to truly benefiting from foreign assistance, not every institution has prepared itself for genuine organic growth. It may have failed to come forward with a practical design for upgrading its faculty, neglected research opportunities, overlooked salary problems, or forgotten about community support. It may be lacking a nucleus of devoted and responsible leaders willing and able to foster institutional growth, if necessary at the expense of their own professional advancement and prestige. There are certain matters that institutions, no less than individuals or nations, cannot leave to chance. What is to be their role in a wider geographic region? How are they to weight numerical growth against the pursuit of excellence? How much or how little should they undertake in a specific field? Is their mission to train the teachers, public servants, engineers, and doctors to serve the nation and other social and educational institutions? Or is their role conceived in more parochial, if worthy, terms of building a civic culture for their immediate constituents? Finally, has the leadership made a fresh and self-critical review of strengths and weaknesses and laid down the broad guidelines for responding to institutional needs? Recog-

130

nizing that its resources are always more restricted than its needs, how far has it gone in establishing priorities for determining points of emphasis next year and three or five years hence?

Partners in institution-building, who can at best assist only a few institutions, cannot escape the obligation to assess the many factors essential to growth. Perhaps what is needed is an institutional equivalent of the pilot's checklist before clearing the aircraft for flight. But in the end, when the many factors essential to growth have been considered, partners must consider the institution as a whole. For whether the aim is developing a university or building a strong and vital research institute, the organization is somehow more than the sum of its parts. Those who assess in order to help must acquire the knack of measuring the potential and strength of institutions in the process of evolving. Universities in some parts of the world are little more than loose collections of faculties. If it is the university that invites development, this fact may lead to their exclusion, or it may require a new approach to institution-building. If outside donor organizations concentrate their resources at a few developing institutions, the corollary of their assistance is single-minded concentration by indigenous leadership on the central problems of institution-building.

A second principle that we can glean from the broad range of private assistance underscores the importance of identifying and defining discreet and manageable areas of assistance. This need is an outgrowth of the essential nature of technical assistance. Outside help is inevitably marginal help. At the peak of the Marshall Plan, the flow of aid never exceeded 4 percent of Europe's capital needs. Private foundations particularly must come to a judicious determination of the focus of their aid. Policies follow questions that go to the heart of cooperative efforts. What are the recipient country's most urgent and pressing needs and what is it doing about them? What is it doing for itself and what does it seek from others? Viewed realistically, what capacity does the donor agency possess, or can it acquire, for assistance in those areas where it can make a genuine difference?

Whether the choice is agriculture or virus research or improving an economics faculty, there are dividends in defining and identifying areas of need and matching them against available outside resources. In Thailand the Rockefeller Foundation has concentrated its efforts in university development on the strengthening of three basic disciplines: medical and basic sciences, agriculture, and economics. Within its operating agricultural programs, the emphasis has been on research and training programs directed toward strengthening various countries' ability to produce certain basic food crops, such as corn, wheat, sorghum, potatoes, and rice. These crops were chosen because they are crucial for specific economies. Thus, corn and wheat have been the focus in Mexico, rice and sorghum in Asia. The goal has been improved varieties and techniques, not across the entire agricultural spectrum, but in areas where need and capacity could be joined. Again, in the Foundation's university development efforts, its focus has been on disciplines ready and able to use assistance for which the sources of intellectual cooperation were in sight.

At some point, when the overall capacity of a nation and its institutions has been developed, it may decide that its major thrust should be, say, in strengthening its capacity to deal with population, or unemployment, or internal migration. At that point, a foundation may wish to concentrate exclusively in a single vital area. But to begin and end with one area can be a case of putting the cart before the horse and can lead to problems of imbalance and uneven progress in ways that exacerbate rather than improve the national picture.

A third principle already adumbrated is the vital importance of continuity. The Rockefeller Foundation's Mexican Agricultural Program was inaugurated in 1943. It has evolved from a limited exploratory effort, through a national program carefully housed in the Office of Special Studies within the Ministry of Agriculture, to the current International Maize and Wheat Improvement Center. Nearly thirty years later, a handful of the original team of Rockefeller Foundation agricultural scientists continue to serve as participant advisors in a fully Mexican international agricultural program, aiming to share with others the accumulated knowledge developed in the past three decades. There is a time to give assistance and a time to withhold it or bring it to an end. The University of the Philippines, under the vital and dynamic leadership of General Carlos P. Romulo, reached the stage, particularly in the arts and sciences, where strategically placed assistance could enable it to move to a new level of excellence. How shortsighted it would have been for agencies that had faithfully provided fellowship help in other periods in its history to have terminated aid at that point. Now, with the growing nationalization of the university the possibilities and need for aid become more restricted and more sharply defined.

Fourth, a career service of men engaged in assistance to developing institutions is essential. The Gardner Report proposed an AID career service backstopped by a cadre of AID reservists. Experiences that hark back to the International Health Division of the Rockefeller Foundation point the way to the maintenance of professional competence for international service. If Henry Wriston is right when he states that first-class problems attract first-class minds, the rallying of qualified personnel should not be impossible. The Rockefeller Foundation, in its University Development Program, has been encouraged by the interest of first-rate scholars in serving abroad as visiting professors, heads of departments, and even deans. Some have been recruited as regular Foundation staff, others as temporary personnel, and others as scholars on leave from their own universities. A career service for university development must be flexible enough to provide for commitments ranging across a sliding scale of interest. Some will be engaged more or less permanently, others for a year or two. It is obvious that any plan for a career service that would attract the best minds must allow for both service and research— the continuation of a scholar's most deeply cherished interests. Essential will be the presence in any organized effort at a university development center of at least a few topflight leaders devoting themselves full-time to academic administration and teaching. Their presence at the heart of the development enterprise leaves room for researchers who teach by carrying forward their inquiries.

In the end, the fate of American education abroad is dependent on responsible and well-qualified people engaged in tasks for which there is recognized need. Sometimes this involves doing well what a scholar is required to do in any educational setting. At other times the adaptation must be more drastic. Perhaps the success of the American educational effort is greatest when the approach is indirect and oblique. American agronomists, economists, or virologists probably contribute most when they labor as scientists and scholars drawing on the full range of knowledge which they can appropriate not because they are Americans, but because of professional competence. If this is the test of American education, it is more likely to be realized within the framework of an organized, concentrated, career-oriented approach to institution-building abroad.

A fifth principle, the corollary of the concept of a career service, is the need to build supplementary structures and arrangements for strengthening institutions abroad. The AID philosophy of sister university relationships was, as John Gardner observed, a creative invention for institution-building, but suffered in its implementation. It was plagued by misunderstandings, mediocrity, and inflexibility, but the heart of the idea was sound. There are by-products of university-to-university cooperation that serve both institutions and their personnel.

The Rockefeller Foundation has made approximately twenty-five university grants to institutions in Britain, France, Canada, Switzerland, and the United States, patterned after the arrangements described in the Gardner Report—but with a difference. First, the universities concerned extend assistance to developing institutions through visiting professors and cooperating junior colleagues in specific disciplines. For example, the Yale Growth Center, the Williams College Institute of Economic Development, and Northwestern University give help in economics. Princeton, Notre Dame, Cornell, Duke, Michigan, Wisconsin, and Minnesota Universities send visitors in the social sciences, as do Toronto, Sussex, and McGill. Second, the developing universities themselves play a determining role in the selection of cooperating Western universities and the choice of individual professors. Third, a schedule is worked out of visitors for successive academic years so that both the developing and developed universities can make plans for the years ahead.

Fourth, the professionals concerned, including career service personnel at the developing universities, play an active role not only in selecting visiting professors but defining their role and working out the most meaningful assignments before they arrive. It would be impossible to exaggerate the pivotal role of the senior foundation representative in planning, consulting, and paving the

136

way for the visitors and assuring they have a serious piece of work to do without wasted time and effort. Fifth, the watchword is flexibility. A particular Western university, principally engaged in strengthening university X, is not precluded from assisting university Y. Equally, university X can receive help from more than one source, if appropriate. Sixth, the role of visitors is part of a total university development plan and their contributions are made to mesh with the overall design.

It is important, finally, to take note of the anatomy of university development according to this approach. It rests on an overall university plan made a prerequisite to any substantial amount of foundation assistance. The planners are educators and administrators in the indigenous university, but the foundation's career officers are commonly invited to join in formulating the plan. From the foundation's side, a distinct and definable plan having a beginning, a middle, and an end is evolved. The design makes provision both for phasing in and phasing out. It characteristically starts modestly, expands to a peak of activity, and phases out on a graduated basis with the local university taking over. For all this there is no copybook scheme concocted in a forty-second floor office in New York City. The anatomy of development is an organic process and those who contribute most are those who see themselves as gardeners, not mechanics. Their initiative is on the ground in relation to forces that cannot be grasped or understood from afar. Without a strategy or plan, however, their work loses its direction and purpose.

137

The final observation, which follows from a sixty-year experience in foreign assistance, is the need for scientists to operate within a framework and to be ever mindful of the interrelatedness of human progress. The successes of foreign assistance create new challenges and problems, some more exacting and serious than the failures. The work of development too often has been a "catch-up" operation. It is probably unfair to say that the success of the IHD created the population explosion—but surely it was a contributing factor. Improved health, lower mortality rates, and longer life spans thereby add to a nation's problems. We see now some of the hazards in pursuing health or agricultural programs in isolation. The unique opportunity that university development presents is that advances on one front can be coordinated with determined and concentrated efforts along other fronts. Programs in improved health delivery systems can go on simultaneously with population control. Efforts to increase food production can be accompanied by inquiries into the economic and social consequences of "the green revolution." Instead of "catching-up" the developing countries can be assisted in preparing for the problems that lie ahead three, five, or ten years down the road.

University development and institution-building is a marvelously flexible and comprehensive instrument, and for those on both sides it can be a framework which in the past has been conspicuously missing.

# 7: THE VALUES BY WHICH
   MEN LIVE

If economic and political projects in international cooperation introduce complexities surpassing those in international scientific cooperation, the uncertainties and intangibles of values are still more baffling—but fundamental. If we look at the anatomy and semantics of values, their form, interaction, and possible definition, we find not one but many concepts, each with different uses and content. Values have many meanings. By values, men sometimes mean the behavior patterns of a particular culture rooted in underlying social goals and purposes. When these patterns are common to many cultures they are described as universal. We also speak of values as social currency—those shared values within a society which make unified action possible because through them men recognize that they have the same aspirations and goals. Values may also take on a transcendent character, giving validity and meaning to national and international life, and self-respect and worth to individuals. Transcendent values afford the basis for social structures, legitimize a society's goals, but also can throw up barriers to change. Finally, there are functional values which serve to maintain a balance between society and its environment. Values are operative at these and other levels, but taken together they constitute organizing principles by which men and nations live, move, and have their being.

## VALUES AND THE AMERICAN EXPERIENCE

The meaning and purpose of values is an especially critical issue for the United States at this moment in our history. In James Reston's words: ". . . the American purpose in the world is very dim and confused these days, even in our own minds, and maybe a restatement or affirmation of that purpose is the first order of business. . . ."[1] However, it is tempting for Americans, having mastered the requirements of large-scale production of goods and services for millions of people, to assume thereby that our place in history is assured and that the world will beat a path to our doorstep. We have been endlessly inventive in scientific output, economic development, and large-scale organization; the products of our economy are broadcast over most of society. We are a privileged people, it is said, and the great masses of the world's underprivileged can share our largess once they appropriate our technical and scientific know-how. Economic development according to this scale of values becomes the first order of business and with it the use of the economy to assure national security through military preparedness.

[1] *New York Times,* November 21, 1971, section IV, p. 13.

Yet it is the whole of our society, not its economic achievements, that is daily subjected to scrutiny from points around the globe. If we are experiencing a "time of testing," that judgment is not focused simply on the rise and fall of gross national product nor on the state of our military establishment. Nevertheless, those who urge that we pay more attention to the techno-scientific aspect of the world crisis are in the ascendancy and have the advantage of appearing to grapple with what is immediate, measurable, and tangible. In speaking to the world's underprivileged, their message appears to lead from strength in the American nation.

In a deeper sense, the world crisis is less a confrontation between national economies and more one between whole societies. What is alarming is not our essential response to the former, but to the latter challenge. It is paradoxical that we gave greater weight to national goals and values than to military and industrial achievements at a time when we were less absorbed with the world's needs. Speaking at Independence Hall in Philadelphia, en route to his inauguration, Abraham Lincoln asked, in effect, what it was that we had to offer the world. What was unique in the American experience and what lessons were embodied in the creation and preservation of the Union? It was not our geographic isolation from the "motherland" but something more. It was, in Lincoln's words, "something in that Declaration giving liberty, not alone to the people of this country, but hope to the world . . . which gave promise that in due time the

141

weights should be lifted from the shoulders of all men. . . ."[2]

It is important to ask what has happened to this first great proposition and the primacy Lincoln accorded it. Why does it sound so quaint and far-removed from present-day discourse? Has it gone the way of those other first principles present at the creation but largely forgotten by a divided people—a people with an uncertain and ambivalent view of themselves and their relations with one another, their allies and adversaries, and the hungry majority of the human race?

The fact is that far from overcoming, we are overawed and ourselves overcome by the magnitude and complexity of our leadership position and the great national and international problems. Despite strenuous and widely heralded efforts, we have not lifted the weights from the shoulders of more than a small portion of mankind. In the process we have come to doubt the values on which our best initiatives have been based. This is why a sense of urgency is attached to reconsidering the values antecedent to and inherent in the American cultural and political heritage. It has become fashionable to proclaim that old values are dying and new ones have not yet been born. The spiritual wellsprings of our heritage include values that may have been more appropriate to a rural or pastoral way of life from a time of sheep and shepherds.

[2] Abraham Lincoln, speech at Independence Hall, Philadelphia, Pennsylvania, February 22, 1861. From *Collected Works of Abraham Lincoln* ed. R. P. Basler (New Brunswick, N.J.: Rutgers University Press, 1953), Vol. IV, p. 240.

Critics question their relevance for a techno-scientific and post-religious age. Practical men of affairs give primacy to prompt action on urgent needs, not to great propositions; to problem-solving, not to high moral principles. And the elements of our history since Woodrow Wilson make it abundantly clear that the factors of social and international life will not yield to a single simplifying proposition, however transcendent. In short, however moral we strive to be, in the personal or collective order, we contend not with one all-informing principle but with competing and proximate principles often in a state of tension and contradiction, and in the eyes of the world we have not come to terms with this.

Yet even if we could convince ourselves that the quest for historic purposes is a will-of-the-wisp, the rest of the world will not allow us this luxury. At international conferences, essentially every day of the year, U.S. representatives are asked "What does America stand for in the world?" Others, not so tactfully, remind us that they are continuously engaged in the quest for their own national identity and challenge our apparent preoccupation with material and technological goals. With the approach of 1976, our embarrassment increases, which is in part at least the motivation for reconsidering our heritage and projecting it into the future. Fortunately, we find evidence that, as has been true throughout our history, first-order problems are attracting first-rate minds: individuals, clusters of individuals working together, and institutionally sponsored endeavors.

However, the best efforts of our best minds will falter

unless we combine a sensitive concern for what is timeless and enduring in our heritage with what is transient and relevant only in the more limited context of time and place. The founding fathers, expressing themselves in documents such as the Federalist Papers, saw this distinction more clearly than some of our contemporary observers. They postulated a series of broad values and principles that comprised the "Higher Law." These specified ultimate values, such as liberty, order, justice and equality, as broad standards and guidelines for specific constitutional and legislative enactments. The Bill of Rights was a concrete and detailed statement, informed and inspired by the "Higher Law." So too were provisions concerning the separation of powers and the limitations of the powers of government. Due process of law and electoral procedures were less specific but still rooted in "higher truth." Moreover, the architects of the Constitution were aware that every detailed provision in the political order must be open to evolution and revision and guaranteed this through provisions for constitutional amendment.

From the beginning, therefore, our leaders distinguished between universal principles and the practical arrangements for implementing or approximating these principles. They were wise men in yet another respect. They knew that in the practical realm, proximate values and goals might conflict and would have to be balanced and harmonized by imperfect men seeking to adjust to changing realities. The problem first arose in the controversy over the powers of central vs. local authority. It

144

reappeared in the debate over executive vs. legislative power. Being practical as well as prophetic in their outlook, the authors of the Constitution recognized such issues could not be settled once and for all—prompting the wry comment by the twentieth-century constitutional lawyer Professor Edwin Corwin that the Constitution was an invitation to continuing civil war between the executive and legislative branches of government.

In the years which followed, constitutionalists and legislators have carved out rulings and interpretations which reflect the inescapable need for balancing ultimate values in their application—liberty and order, peace and national security, freedom and justice, liberty and equality. Confronted with new and urgent problems, they chose to emphasize now one and then another value or principle in the interests of a better society. What was never forgotten in most of these applications was Chief Justice Marshall's reminder that "It is a Constitution we are interpreting!" In the language of this discussion, we can substitute higher values for Constitution, for it was these values from which the Constitution drew and sustained its legitimacy.

It has been well said that he who engages in defining and applying values and goals resembles a juggler. He must be ever alert to the fact that he works with multiple, not single, values, and that the whole must be kept in balance while the relative weights and positions change constantly. In the real world, whether that of the family or the nation, he deals with not one good and worthy purpose, but many. No one has resolved once and for

145

all how values are interrelated. It is part of the moral and political task to relate them afresh and in terms of a higher principle such as justice, defined as giving each man his due. And in the political order, he pursues his task in the face of interests and pressures that arise in the body politic and require judgment on what is possible as well as desirable.

Whatever the dilemmas and complexities of implementing "higher values" and giving them specific content, no society has freed itself from the need for reflection on and application of values. There are no value-free societies, however imperfect the "legislators" of values may be in bringing them into force or approximating them in practice. Every society has need for men and leaders who make "an unusually stubborn attempt to think clearly"[3] about values. And the United States—at its birth and no less in the present—has need to be ever vigilant to the values and goals that inform its national and international life.

## VALUES AND CULTURES

The heart of the value question as it touches international relations has to do with the interaction and penetration of cultures by internal and external values. Recently, cultural interaction has been seen in the context of a world in which the West (including the USSR) was the producer and creator of the goods and values of mod-

---

[3] William James's definition of philosophy.

ern civilization and traditional cultures were simple consumers. The real issue is how to involve the larger part of the world in a world civilization in which they are not doomed to be mere consumers of goods produced by the industrially more advanced cultures. Economic development in this sense is not simply taking industrial production to the poorer countries of the world but creating tasks and employment that give men the kind of pride essential to their functioning as creative and social individuals.

Viewed in this light, traditional cultures ought not be seen as obsolescent phenomena or anachronisms that history has decreed must and will disappear. The high cost of the destruction of a traditional culture is often overlooked. If traditional culture disappears, what is sometimes left is a spiritual vacuum, with accompanying social alienation and human decay, leading to anti-social behavior, conflict, and withdrawal. An example of this is the fate of the Bantus taken out of their tribal setting in South Africa. Cultures become passive and too often indifferent acceptors of the cultural products of others. They become objects for the actions of others, not initiators and creative forces in their own right.

Those who promote international cooperation between cultures must adopt a sense of urgency about the relevance of traditional culture because: (1) It is the reality in which a large part of mankind is rooted. (2) It constitutes the baseline from which these societies can modernize and develop responses and institutions enabling them to relate to the rest of the world on some basis of equality and effectiveness. (3) The process of healthy organic growth has to start with precepts that emerge from traditional cultures rather than being pulled and shaped by precepts that come from the outside. (4) Inasmuch as the present world yearns for more than cosmopolitan culture offers and inasmuch as present levels of affluence in the West are not achievable for the poorer, more heavily populated regions of the world, men will have to search for a new and different relation between technology, society and mankind. (5) While some small, unified and isolated cultures have been able to develop economically by being "plugged into" the international system of trade and industry, development cannot occur in this way in the larger, more heterogeneous societies. Even if they "plug in," the effects cannot touch more than a small segment of the whole society. In a word, Indonesia and India are not England or Japan. What such countries need is a way of mobilizing the whole social system and making it capable of self-motivated social transformation. Otherwise these societies will remain stagnant consumers of the cultural and mechanical products of more-advanced countries. To resuscitate the vitality of a nation one must appeal to and revive the values, drives, motivations, and goals that are the wellspring of that civilization.

Having recognized the persistent and essential role of traditional culture, the problem is how to make this discovery operational. In large part, responsibility rests with the developing societies themselves, whose task is one of self-renewal. Traditional societies must reexamine, reevaluate, and reorient ancient values to cope with problems of modernity without paralyzing or tearing

148

themselves apart. They must do this without the relatively long period of comparative isolation the Japanese enjoyed in their successful emergence. While they cannot afford to isolate themselves, they must reject as too high a price for modernization the overburdening presence of a powerful external force which would freeze them into a permanent position of being mere consumers. They must balance the demands for change with the need to hold on to elements of traditional structure and identity while using these deeply rooted traditions to generate motivation across the wide expanse of a populous nation. It is essential for them to remember they deal with numerous clusters of underdevelopment, not a few pockets of misery and poverty. And this approach is possible only by appealing to and reviving historic values, drives, and goals, and recasting them in modern terms. Cosmopolitan cultures can cover only a limited range—the elite—as they provide human potentialities and strive to meet the needs in their societies. Traditional cultures can play a role by bringing new elements into cosmopolitanism, particularly in areas in which man copes with daily life and the ultimate questions of life and death.

On its side, foreign technical assistance and international cooperation can contribute by increasing cultural relativity in the training of people from these developing nations. An individual must be taught a scholarly discipline and modern skills with awareness that the growth of such disciplines is inevitably linked with perceptions and preoccupations in the countries in which they have evolved. Thus when a young economist returns home, he should carry not only American or British orientations to his field, but sensitivity to the contextual aspects of his field inherent in his own culture.

At the same time, our friends in Asia and Africa, in their candor, have counseled that we cannot avoid value conflicts. Those who devise development programs must not be timid. It is as wrong for a donor country to practice false humility as to claim infallibility. We must give assistance not in the spirit of "we are here to help you" but "here is what we have," addressed "to whom it may concern." At some point inescapably we will give offense and all parties must be braced for this. The problem of the catalyst is to trigger renewed vitality; this cannot be done softly. It takes place through challenge, confrontation, and even conflict. If some cultures are unable to grow and change, they will disintegrate. This is not the end of the world. The process must be one of disseminating new values and reinterpreting old values in the new context. It could be that the greatest crime perpetrated by the British in the new African countries was denying them the possibility of fighting for their independence. India, Indonesia, and the Philippines gained national identity through such an encounter. Someone has said, "it is a terrible thing to have a reasonable father."

## VALUES AND AMERICAN POWER

The unique challenge that lies before the United States is to act so that it neither overestimates nor underestimates its impact on history nor its capacity for good or evil. It must learn to live with the fact that American civilization, with all its strengths, is not the best civilization for all time nor the most virtuous but partakes of the many-sided attributes of a long line of past world civilizations. Our consciousness of our mortality may make it easier for others to join us as true partners— provided we retain a sense of identity and direction.

The burdens involved in the exercise of great power are more awesome than the powerful ever fully grasp— particularly if power is linked with a missionary impulse. It is possible for most of us to count on the fingers of one hand the individuals we have known who use their power with dignity, compassion, and strength. In serving the world, we need to keep this human reality ever before us. In international cooperation, the whole world is not our oyster to be captured and exploited. It is more than a field for unilateral research. It is rich soil for joint cooperative ventures and this is our best guideline for cultural relations in the future.

Some would say this is a counsel of perfection in the present world. National self-righteousness is a powerful motivating force behind many programs of technical assistance; the idea of an American Century is not dead. Indeed the paradox of technical assistance today is that generous programs of aid assume a certain attitude of cultural and technological superiority. Yet ironically, if carried to its extreme a renewal of the informing spirit of the white man's burden is the best guarantee of failure abroad, even though it may help build political coalitions at home. Not by accident, the largest expenditures of foreign aid have been prompted by ideological bias. Opposition to communism around the world was the rallying cry for both the Marshall Plan and Truman Doctrine, and for the Russians their hope of expanding the Communist sphere of influence was the dominant motivation of most of the aid given by the USSR. The same is undoubtedly true of the great increase in Chinese foreign aid in the past year or so. Witnesses with long experience before committees of the Congress privately acknowledge that in testifying they deliberately invoked crusading anti-Communist arguments to gain support, while being convinced in their hearts that positive reasons for economic development represented a sounder appeal. The long legislative history of linking foreign economic aid to military assistance is but the most tangible and explicit evidence of the strength of this deep-seated trend.

It can be argued that the tide is turning and that "the great simplifiers" who see the world divided into two huge lumps of mankind have become less convincing with each passing year. There are supporting trends, such as the rise of the "third world" owing allegiance neither to east nor west, which lend credence to this changing viewpoint. Major studies of foreign aid such as "the Pearson Report" view the world in more sophisticated and realistic terms, calling for a positive development approach akin to the spirit of the U.N. Development Decade. Nonetheless, there are counterforces at work in the emerging isolationism in the U.S. and some European countries.

152

## The Values by Which Men Live

The world's problems are numerous and varied: food shortages, overpopulation, marginal men desperately struggling for existence on the fringes of the cities, the threat of a thermonuclear holocaust, and the spread of environmental deterioration. The answers to these problems and others that lie ahead rest not with incantations or slogans. It will not do to invoke pious creeds that leave the basic problems untouched and the miserably starving and hard-pressed masses unmoved.

Yet, the problem of publics in the donor countries is also a stubborn reality. Men are not moved to sacrifice their treasure, blood, sweat, and tears by narrowly pragmatic appeals. In the present stage of international relations, loyalty to the nation-state and its goals takes primacy. The adage still applies: "What I cannot do as an individual, I realize vicariously through the grandeur and deeds of the nation." Highly tentative and severely qualified statements about national goals generate loyalty from a handful of professional observers but seldom from the public at large. One has only to compare public attitudes during World War I toward "a war to end wars" with responses by Americans in the Vietnam War to calls to resist nations "who will not leave their neighbors alone."

If this is a counsel of despair to those who call for educated and informed approaches to foreign assistance, the answer for the long-run must be "educate the people." The warm-hearted, compassionate, and international-minded people who make up the American public are capable of seeing the international crisis in perspective.

Americans are problem-solvers, as de Tocqueville saw them—especially the young, whose idealism may yet be harnessed to concrete, defined, and singular goals. Historically there has been a deeply moral commitment to helping others, and no postwar administration has tapped this fast-running stream in American life. We are a religious and moral people, not perhaps in organized and institutionalized terms but, as James Reston reminds us, as heirs of the residual Judeo-Christian heritage. Some day national leaders will speak to these feelings and goals and foreign assistance will be raised to a higher, more inspiring plane, less divisive and confusing to the rest of the world.

Even in practical political terms, a stronger justification is possible. The only absolutes in our national life are "the higher principles" in which our constitutional guarantees are rooted: justice, equality, liberty, order. In practical political terms, any specific policy or social arrangement is at best an approximation of these higher goals, or an instrument which by trial and error we judge is calculated to lead to such goals. The tendency in recent American politics has been to absolutize the institutions or machinery by which we pursue higher ends, confusing thereby ends and means in a society which, like all societies, is sometimes but not always virtuous.

In a nutshell, our problem is that by casting our working institutions and practical political arrangements as absolutes we complicate relationships with the rest of the world. We are uncompromisingly self-righteous about proximate moral and political "solutions," whereas our moral fervor ought to be reserved for broad overarching

154

national purposes that others can recognize and respect as universals. The lesson of the postwar world is that Communist and non-Communist societies, developed and underdeveloped nations alike have practical problems that each must resolve within a national and cultural context. It serves no purpose to argue on a take it or leave it basis about institutional arrangements if thereby we close out the possibility of working together for common needs and mutual interests. The late Winston Churchill often quoted the Duke of Marlborough who wrote: "Interests never lie." It is in the interest of all nations around the world that their peoples be fed rather than hungry, housed rather than destitute, educated rather than ignorant, and capable of managing their urgent problems on an orderly and peaceful basis. Significantly, their interests and successes are in our interest as well, for the conflicts that have broken out in the postwar world have occurred, not within nations that had their problems in hand, but those that were badly divided over failures to cope with urgent social and political demands. Given the costs of waging wars once the conflicts have erupted and violence replaced the orderly processes of social change, the cost-benefits of foreign assistance should be obvious to rich and poor nations alike.

## VALUES AND FOREIGN AID

What is needed, even assuming this radical shift in political thinking (which remains a hope and not a reality in the present), are success stories in foreign assis-

155

tance or models of international cooperation. Who can doubt, given the complexities and uncertainties of politically based programs, that this constitutes a fertile and promising field for private initiative. For it is in this arena that risk-taking is proper and necessary, sustained and painstaking experiments or pilot projects can go forward, and projects be judged by results, not nationalistic proof-tests.

In a day when many doubt the efficacy of foreign aid, those who would innovate on a larger scale must see targets of opportunity that can be realistically pursued. We need more "Mexican Agricultural Programs"—both because the developing countries have staggering and overwhelming problems to be solved and because we need a rebirth of confidence in our capacity to give meaningful assistance. Foreign assistance has a bad image because not enough is known about what can be and has been accomplished. Too often bad experiences alone make news.

Private efforts, moreover, can play a role during the period of self-examination and reevaluation through which we as a nation are moving. Ironically, in the aftermath of the national self-righteousness that had come to dominate some of our efforts we now have entered a period of moral perplexity and self-doubt. We have come to doubt our own values, in part because we have been prone to confuse stratagems and tactical moves with our underlying values. We have sanctified our moves on the chessboard of international politics and confused them with the values by which we live. What was provisionally necessary for a great power caught up in the Cold War has been equated with those essentials of our moral tradition derived from two thousand years of experience with the evolving challenges that must be met by actions based on a profound understanding of the true nature of man.

As we strive to recover and reformulate our national goals in the world and restate lasting values, private undertakings in international cooperation can help to bridge the gulf. They can proceed free of the pressures and compulsions that limit and constrain public efforts. We can buy time for genuine cooperative efforts in the public sector by demonstrating what is possible in the private sector. And if the day ever comes when the public sector can appropriate and carry forward, with larger resources and manpower, the lessons of private groups, these same free and independent groups who remain central to the American tradition can redirect energies and skills to areas still untouched by public endeavors, which for every era almost certainly will demand more resources and human skills than are available to meet the challenge. For the story of international cooperation is inescapably one of challenge and response, with urgent needs and unsolved problems almost always exceeding the resources of the day. This is the human drama in which we are destined to play out our brief but all-important roles. A view from the private sector may help us to do our part and, if so, the goal of this little book will have been realized.

157

# INDEX